HUMANITY
Patrick Bonneville Society

CITIES

D0012626

KIM MURRAY
WITH SHANNON PARTRIDGE
AND PATRICK BONNEVILLE

HUMANITY
Patrick Bonneville Society

CITIES

THE WORLD'S TOP 100 MEANINGFUL CITIES

DESIGNED BY
PATRICK BONNEVILLE

This book is dedicated to all New Yorkers.
You won my heart a long time ago.

Patrick Bonneville

Published by
PATRICK BONNEVILLE SOCIETY
310 Parmenter, Sutton, Quebec
J0E 2K0 Canada
www.patrickbonneville.ca

Writer: Kim Murray
Research: Kim Murray, Patrick Bonneville
Editor: Shannon Partridge
Proofreading: Kelli Ann Ferrigan
Designer: Patrick Bonneville
Consultant designer: Philippe Hemono

Cover design: Patrick Bonneville
Back cover text: Shannon Partridge
Half title page: Cpenler/Dreamstime.com
Full title page: Simona Dumitru/Dreamstime.com
Introduction: Jenny Solomon/Dreamstime.com

The publisher offers special thanks to
Kim Murray, Shannon Partridge, Kelli
Ann Ferrigan, Gina Garza, Lori Baird,
Isabelle Paradis and Philippe Hemono.
The publisher also thanks Céline
Laprise, Caroline Leclerc and Louis
Dubé from the SODEC. *Merci à tous.*

Printed and bound in China

ISBN 978-1-926654-06-5

Legal deposit - Bibliothèques et Archives
nationales du Québec, 2010

Legal deposit - Library and Archives
Canada, 2010

First edition

Series created by Patrick Bonneville

Produced with the support of Quebec
Refundable Tax Credit for Book Production
Services and Sodexport program.

SODEC
Québec

"When you look at a city, it's like reading the hopes, aspirations and pride of everyone who built it."
—*Architect Hugh Newell Jacobsen*

CONTENTS

Photo credit: Angela Campanelli

Cities are the soul of humanity. They are our greatest achievements, in engineering, architecture, and planning. They are the cradle of our cultures, our educational institutions, and our economic systems. Human ingenuity has overcome all kinds of natural obstacles to erect our cities. In our cities, humans have learned the art of compromise that is required to merge tribal or clan affinities with those of others. Sometimes more successfully than others, we have learned to live in community with people we don't know and likely never will.

Humans didn't always converge in cities. For the first time in history, most of the people on Earth now live in urban centers. It is where we meet, where we work, where we create, and where we change the world.

Not all big cities are great, though. While some have been able to manage their growth with planning and organization, others have had difficulties in adapting to the heavy migration of those fleeing rural poverty. Nor have all big cities have played an important role in our collective history. Not all big cities have inspired us, made us dream, survived revolutions, or changed the world for the better. Some are great collectives of poverty and destitution. Others are enclaves of violence and division.

This book about the best of the best cities: the ones that we love, the ones that have left a mark on humanity or are doing so right now. They are the cities we might all want to visit at least once in our lives.

Patrick Bonneville

The Ranking Process

Many publishing folk and friends have asked me about the top-100 format of the HUMANITY books. Why do we choose a subjective ranking process? Well, here is my most honest answer: we want to make a statement. By listing these cities we can put emphasis on the ones we think are worth the most attention.

Ranking also creates debate and discussion. We want people to talk about what cities are the greatest and for what reasons. Ranking leads us to challenge and defend what is important to us and to humanity. Ranking the cities of the world helps us better imagine the kind of cities we want to create and live in.

On the other hand, our ranking is certainly not absolute truth. We acknowledge our Western bias, which might very well play a big role in this book. We have visited some cities more often than others; we read and hear more about some than others too. We also acknowledge the limitations of our research—obviously the best way to evaluate a city is to visit it and all its neighborhoods. And obviously, and regrettably, we were unable to do that.

We chose to apply five criteria in ranking the cities:

Well-being
What is the quality of life in the city? How safe is it? How are the basic services?

Historical Role
What role did it play in its nation's history or in world history?

Attraction
Are people attracted to this city? How many foreign visitors visit every year?

Population
How large is the city? How many people live in the metropolitan area?

Dynamism
Does the city have a dynamic culture and economy?

"These have been hard times. We have been drawn across the knife-edge of poverty. We have been shaken by troubles that would have destroyed any other city. But we are not any other city. We are the city of New York and New York in adversity towers above any other city in the world."
—*Edward Irving Koch, Mayor of New York City from 1978 to 1989*

Patrick Bonneville: Many of you would agree with me that if we had to choose one city as the capital of the world, New York would probably be it. New York is what the word "city" is all about. New York is where the world meets—not just as the financial center of the world, but also because it represents the dynamism of ethnicity from all corners of the planet; all these cultures are alive within one single, great city. New York was built by the Dutch, English, Irish, Italians, Scottish, Germans, French, Russians, Chinese, Indians, Hispanics, Africans, Amerindians; it was built by people from every point on the compass.

On September 11, 2001, when the terrorists hit the Twin Towers, they got it wrong if they wanted to hurt Americans. By hitting New York that day, they hurt all of us, citizens of the world. That day we were all New Yorkers.

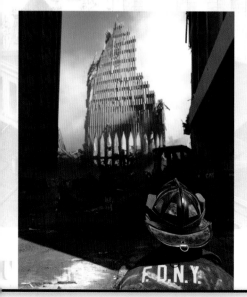

Known a few hundred years ago as New Amsterdam, the city was settled by the Dutch as a fur-trading center. In 1624 its population was only 270, but there was great hope for the future of the city. The British saw this and conquered the area and baptized the land "New York" in 1664. Not to be outdone, the Dutch re-conquered the city in 1673. They renamed it New Orange, or *Nieuwe Oranje,* in honor of the Dutch Prince of Orange, who would become King William of England. Eventually, a deal was made and into the history books it went as the British traded Suriname (a country in South America) for the New Netherland region, which included Manhattan Island.

Time rolled on and people rolled in. The port and immigration center at Ellis Island is a symbol of new beginnings. It received would-be Americans from all around the world, their eyes full of wonder, their hearts full of hope. The city grew, and grew, and grew! People built upwards and skyscrapers emerged as quickly as spring buds on a tree.

"Tomorrow New York is going to be here. And we're going to rebuild, and we're going to be stronger than we were before...I want the people of New York to be an example to the rest of the country, and the rest of the world, that terrorism can't stop us."
—Mayor Rudy Giuliani, 9/11, 2001

CONNECTING THE CITIES OF NEW YORK AND BROOKL

Columbia University was founded in 1754 (known then as King's College in Lower Manhattan). In 1788, New York City was crowned the first capital of the United States. It was the birthplace of the United States Bill of Rights and the home of the first US Supreme Court. On April 30, 1789, President George Washington was inaugurated at Federal Hall on Wall Street.

World War I and II began and ended and New York City's popularity grew. Veterans and immigrants flocked by the thousands to NYC and formed neighborhoods like Chinatown, Little Italy, Little Manila, and Koreatown. Its current population is a true melting pot of cultures, with people from over 100 countries speaking more than 170 languages. Today, New York City's population is about thirty-six percent foreign-born.

With so many people settling in so short a time, the city was an easy target for corruption and crime. By the time Fiorello LaGuardia was a young man, the city was in need of a strong leader. He ran for the mayor's office and lost his first bid in 1923, but in 1933, New York City was ready for this pint-sized giant. His vow was to "clean house and clean it thoroughly." His first radio address was clear: "New York City was restored to the people this morning at one minute after midnight. It is my duty from now on to guard and protect and guide the complete, peaceful and undisturbed enjoyment of that possession." He spent twelve years fulfilling his promises and left the city with a respectable government and a good, solid base for the future.

The city's multicultural climate is an important source of nourishment for the arts and financial sectors. The four major U.S. television networks are all headquartered in New York: ABC, CBS, FOX and NBC.

Far left: September 11, 2001. 343 New York firefighters lost their lives that day.
Left: On August 14th, 1945, following the end of World War II, photographer Alfred Eisenstaedt immortalized V-Day celebrations in Times Square.

Well-being	9/10
Historical role	8.5/10
Attraction	10/10
Population	10/10
Dynamism	10/10
Average score	9.5/10

"The great city is that which has the greatest man or woman: if it be a few ragged huts, it is still the greatest city in the whole world."
—New Yorker and journalist Walter Whitman

Forty-seven million tourists visit New York City every year. They might visit one of the more than two thousand arts and cultural organizations and events or perhaps drop by one of the five hundred art galleries. Maybe they'll ride to the top of a high-rise—one of 5,538—or be one of the 75,000 people who take the free Staten Island Ferry every day or visit the Statue of Liberty. Tourists are comforted by the lowest crime rate of all major U.S. cities, and 25 million of them stroll through Central Park each year. There, they can join New Yorkers in the 843-acre park as they go jogging, have a picnic, do some bird watching, or sit by one of the fifty water fountains or monuments or 36 bridges and archways.

New York City has always seen itself as a modern metropolis. City planners embraced the industrial revolution; it would become the foundation for important transportation routes. Elevated trains were introduced in early 1867. In 1904, the first subway became operational, with 150,000 New Yorkers hopping on board that first day. The subway cost five cents in 1904 and the fare remained the same for 42 years. Today, public transit is the first choice for many New Yorkers; more than fifty percent of the population uses public transit daily.

The United Nations is headquarted in New York City. The flag of every member nation greets you as you pass. Each flag could just as easily represent the multitude of cultural groups who make New York home.

Left: Times Square.

New York has the most important port complex on the East Coast of North America. The Port Authority of New York and New Jersey controls seven cargo terminals. Each offers highly structured shipping services including rail, ocean and land. The port is at the hub of the most concentrated and affluent consumer market in the world: all business eyes turn to New York.

New York is the number one choice, according to *BusinessWeek*, for where Americans want to work and live. It is also a desirable home for artists of all disciplines. And why not? The city has around-the-clock entertainment, endless professional opportunities, extensive public transportation and Central Park!

The stereotypes seem true: a New Yorker is hardworking and kind, and there is a brotherhood that extends beyond boroughs. The city is defined by justice, freedom, and yellow cabs. New York is the city that never sleeps, the city of dreams, the city that inspires. It is the city that gives love and gets love. New York City is a city of humanity.

The *Global Cities Index* is a ranking of cities that confirms the physical manifestation of the world's urban pull. It is assembled by foreign policy and management consultants A. T. Kearney and the Chicago Council. New York City is their choice for number one.

"New York is the greatest place on earth."
—*John Lennon*

"If you are lucky enough to have lived in Paris as a young man, then wherever you go for the rest of your life, it stays with you, for Paris is a movable feast."
—*Ernest Hemingway*

Left: Author Kim Murray and her son in Paris.
Right: Gargoyle on the Notre Dame cathedral.

Patrick Bonneville: In my opinion, Paris is by far the most beautiful city. It has been carved and sculpted with great care through the ages. A walk in Paris is like a walk in a museum. For someone from the New World, like me, this kind of history seems nearly impossible. No wonder Parisians are proud!

We almost lost Paris during World War II when Hitler wanted to blow up everything near the Seine; the world would have turned gray for eternity if this had happened. We need Paris for our soul and for romance.

The City of Light has a 2,500-year history. What is now known as Paris's *Ile de la Cité* was originally settled by a Gallic people known as the Parisii, who fished along the shores of the Seine. The Romans conquered the city in 52 BC and built defensive walls around it. Originally named Lutetia by the Gallo-Romans, in 212 AD the city was given its current name.

It is safe to say that Paris has seen its fair share of battles. The city was ruled by the Franks, then the Vikings and Carolingians, and eventually by the Capetian, Valois, and Bourbon dynasties. Paris was the center of action and radical change during the French Revolution of 1789-99, during which the monarchy was snuffed out in favor of a republic. The years of bloody revolution ended with the rise of Napoleon Bonaparte and his First Empire, and with the creation of The Third Republic in 1870, Paris became the capital of the democratic republic we know today as France.

La Ville-Lumière got its famous nickname when it became the first city in Europe to install gaslights on major thoroughfares. The name is also thought to reflect the centrality of Paris during the Age of Enlightenment, when philosophers, artists, and scientists frequented salons to boast of their ideas.

Parisian architecture is unique in Europe. In contemplating the Paris skyline from the roof of a tall building or from a "fly boat" on the Seine, there is no chance of mistaking the city for any other. From the Gothic dimensions of Notre Dame cathedral and the Romanesque rounded steeples of the Basilique du Sacré-Coeur de Montmartre, to the uniform Hausmann-style apartments and shops that line the boulevards, each building whispers a history that is rich, diverse, and perhaps sweetened with a bit of wine.

Modern Paris is respected the world over for its commercial, industrial, and cultural life. It is a magnet for writers and poets, intellects and artists, and for those who dream of such a life. City dwellers might travel to work on Paris's superb transit system, and visitors beware: some merchants might still close their shops for the midday meal! Parisians are known for their *joie de vivre* and can be observed savoring the best of French gastronomy at trendy bistros or enjoying a book or a playful outing at any of a vast array of parks and gardens, such as the 2,090-acre Bois de Boulogne, or the peaceful gravel-pathed Jardin de Luxembourg.

Dozens of city squares feature monuments that attest to the willingness of Parisians to die for freedom and democracy in France's various upheavals. Place de la République and Place de la Bastille mark the idealism of the French Revolution. The humanitarian efforts of Parisians also dot the city. The Hôtel des Invalides, a hospital for aged and crippled soldiers, was initiated by Louis XIV in the 1670s. Fewer than 100 patients now reside in the hospital, which is today a center for paraplegics.

The Louvre Museum is one of the most respected in the world. Used as a palace until 1672, it now houses a vast collection of art from every era. Thousands of visitors pass each day in front of such famous works as the Mona Lisa and the Venus de Milo. Parisians might enjoy a free evening art history class offered at the Louvre, or a demi-tasse of strong coffee at a sidewalk café bordering the museum's public square. The Louvre Pyramid, a glass structure, was constructed above the visitors' center in 1988 and caused an uproar amongst traditionalists. But time has proven that the old and the new can co-exist in Paris with great flair.

The most illustrious shopping district of Europe, the Champs-Elysées is frequented by wealthiest wallets of the world. Tourists also love to walk this stretch, stopping at the shops to admire the *prêt à porter* and sipping *café au lait*. At the top end of the boulevard is a 450-foot circle with twelve avenues radiating from the center. Once known as the Place de l'Étoile, today it is named Place Charles de Gaulle and features the imposing Arc de Triomphe. The arch was commissioned by Napoleon in 1806 and currently houses a monument to the Unknown Soldier, who was buried under the arch on Armistice Day in 1920. True to Paris's democratic fabric, a different patriotic group lights the flame of remembrance each evening.

75 million tourists embrace the City of Love each year. It is one of the most visited cities in the world. Over 200,000,000 people have made the trip to the Eiffel Tower, and countless visitors have feasted upon fresh croissants, braved the traffic roundabouts, and enjoyed late-evening dining that are synonymous with the city.

According to the statistics desk at the Paris Office of Tourism, the number one tourist destination is not the Eiffel Tower; nor is it the Louvre, nor Notre Dame cathedral. It is Disneyland. Kids do rule the roost!

We love Paris for the flair and color it brings to the world.

"We, writers, painters, sculptors, architects, passionate lovers of the beauty, until now intact, of Paris, hereby protest with all our might, with all our indignation, in the name of French taste gone unrecognized, in the name of French art and history under threat, against the construction, in the very heart of our capital, of the useless and monstrous Eiffel Tower, that public spite, often marked by good sense and a spirit of justice, has already been baptized the Tower of Babel."
—*Letter published in* Le Temps, *1887*

Opposite page: Equestrian statue of Jeanne d'Arc at Place des Pyramides in the 1st *arrondissement.* Jeanne d'Arc, national heroine of France, led the French army to victory during the Hundred Years' War.
Left: Adolf Hitler proudly standing in front of the Eiffel Tower, June 23, 1940. Five years later, on August 25, 1945, German military governor of Paris Dietrich von Choltitz disobeyed Hitler's orders to destroy the French capital and surrended the city.

Well-being	9/10
Historical role	10/10
Attraction	10/10
Population	9/10
Dynamism	9/10
Average score	9.4/10

CITY OF

NOS

E

ONDON

"What is the city but the people?"
—William Shakespeare

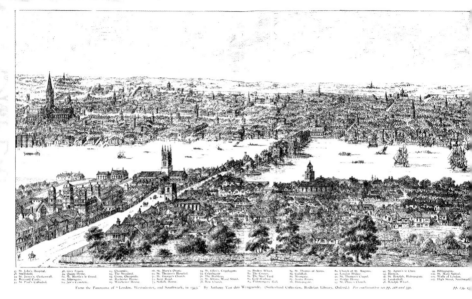

From the Panorama of "London, Westminster, and Southwark, in 1543." By Anthony Van den Wyngaerde. (Sutherland Collection, Bodleian Library, Oxford.)

Patrick Bonneville: The city of kings and queens has had a powerful influence on the rest of the world. Well isolated on its island, London is today a gorgeous mega-city that is home to newcomers from dozens of cultures beyond the sea. The city is infamously expensive to live in, yet life can be beautiful here. London is the solid rock of all cities.

Well-being	9.5/10
Historical role	10/10
Attraction	9/10
Population	9/10
Dynamism	9/10
Average score	9.3/10

London's long history as a city and as the seat of the British Empire accounts for its status among the great cities of the world. Settled in 47 AD by the Romans, this center was then known as Londinium. Although there is no consensus on the origins of the word, many believe it to be from the Celtic *lond*, meaning "wild." If so, it is a fitting description for the changes London has seen through monarchical changeovers, industrialization, and urban sprawl. Today, the metropolitan population is close to 14,000,000.

When the Romans pulled out of England in 410 AD, they left behind a

London with little hope of self-defence and an indigenous population that retained few of the precision and planning skills that the Romans had brought. What happened over the next one hundred years is sketchy. Some historians believe that England fell into ruins and became vulnerable to attacks by the Gauls or other "barbarians." Others believe that economic distress was isolated throughout parts of the territory but not widespread. One thing is agreed, however: London was strategically situated and destined for growth, and by the late 600s, history begins to mention the trading post called Londonwic.

With the unification of the Anglo-Saxon kingdoms in the tenth century, a long series of royal houses would hold the heart and land of England. London's skyline was sculpted by the benificence and vaingloriousness of many of them. Edward the Confessor consecrated an early version of Westminster Abbey in 1065, and William the Conquerer, who reigned after the Norman invasion of 1066, built the Tower of London's central White Tower. His son, William Rufus, built Westminster Palace's great hall, future home of the Palace of Westminster and the royal residence.

Various versions of London Bridge have been built and destroyed in the last 2,000 years. Legend has it that the children's song "London Bridge is Falling Down" was inspired by the 1014 destruction of the timber bridge in an effort to restore the Danish-ruled city to the Anglo-Saxon kings. The permanent Old London Bridge, made of stone, was begun in 1176; it was the only bridge to cross the River Thames until 1739. It was taken down and rebuilt in 1832. During its 650-year service as a link between London and Southwick, there were up to half a million people in the city and surrounding areas. It boggles the mind to imagine a medieval traffic jam upon this narrow bridge lined with houses and shops. King John, who ruled from 1199 to 1216, had ordered these multilevel constructions to be built to fund its maintenance.

In 1215, King John gave city dwellers the right to elect their own mayor from London's aldermen; the leader's role was based upon the French *maire*. Because of the severe crowding and timber constructions of early London, destruction by fire was rampant. During his mandate as the city's first officially recorded mayor, around the turn of the thirteenth century, Henry FitzAilwyn decreed that constructions be raised in stone; this way, loss from fire would be limited. Unfortunately, as history later proved, his decree was mostly ignored.

Upper left: London in the 16th century. This drawing by Anthony van den Wyngaerde is called "Panorama of London." It portrays London at the time of Queen Elizabeth I, William Shakespeare and the race to colonize the New World.

In another significant era of medieval London, religious orders began a building spree that not only beautified the cityscape but offered salvation and succor to the city's many poor. Old St Paul's Cathedral was considered a wonder of the world, and the Southwark Cathedral still stands today. Grand Episcopal palaces and royal mansions were built along the Strand, a street of mansions running parallel to the River Thames. Some lasting secular legacies of this time are Guildhall, built in the early 1400s and the City of London's administrative seat for many centuries, and the Savoy Palace, on the site of today's Savoy Hotel.

The Middle Ages also saw great devastation in London with the arrival of the bubonic plague in 1348. Spread by rats into England along trade routes, the "pestilence" laid waste to the population of the unsanitary and overcrowded city. Some 30,000 of the 70,000 inhabitants succumbed. Those affected developed blackish and bulbous nodes of infection on the neck, and the disease came to be known as the "Black Death." Many Londoners believed the Apocalypse had come, as those they had breakfasted with were buried by nightfall.

The Tudor period was a time of great symbolic change for Londoners. After a thousand years of obedience to papal authority, in the English Reformation of 1534, King Henry VIII caused the separation of English royal authority from that of Rome. His objective in doing so was to secure the anullment of his marriage to Queen Catherine of Aragon in order to marry Anne Boleyn, in hopes that she could provide him with a male heir.

Royal subjects now owed allegiance to King Henry not only as their head of state but as Head of the Church of England. Henry's legacy includes Hyde Park, which served at the time for his own private hunting grounds, and Whitehall Palace, the extravagantly large mansion to which he moved the royal residence in 1530. He is most notorious, however, as the brash and self-indulgent king revealed in the rhyme, "King Henry the Eighth, to six wives he was wedded: one died, one survived, two divorced, two beheaded."

Above: Queen Elizabeth I ruled England from 1558 to 1603. She was born on September 7 1533 in the Greenwich district. Her body was buried at Westminster Abbey after her death in 1603.

During the rule of Queen Elizabeth I, from 1558-1603, and that of her successor King James, London began to thrive. The city was a magnet for writers, poets, actors and painters. As feudalsim declined, citizens were granted the right to own land, and with land ownership came money and spending and individual worth. Trade from the continent and beyond developed, and wealthy Londoners spent their money on such things as French wine, Italian cheeses, and Mediterranean herbs. In part, the love of foreign cuisine was owed to the royal family and their marriages to foreign monarchs. The other part of that recipe consisted of the exotic flavors introduced to Londoners by the growing numbers of immigrants arriving in the city.

Under the reign of Charles II, London nearly ceased to exist. During the London Plague in the summer and fall of of 1665, the Black Death returned to destroy one fifth of the city's population—an estimated 60,000 people. Continuing the city's run of bad luck, the Great Fire of London began on September 2, 1666. At one o'clock on Sunday morning, an easterly wind carried the flames from Pudding Lane in the south to other parts of the city. The inferno lasted until the following Thursday, feeding itself upon some 60 percent of the city. Old St Paul's Cathedral was destroyed, along with eighty-seven parish churches, forty-four livery company halls, and the Royal Exchange.

The face of London changed. The Rebuilding of London Act 1666 stated, "building with brick [is] not only more comely and durable, but also more safe against future perils of fire." From then on, only door cases, window frames and shop fronts were made of wood. The city was rebuilt and soon surpassed Amsterdam as the world's leading financial center. By the eighteenth century, London was one of the most important cities in the world and by the nineteenth century, it was the world's largest port.

At its peak, the British Empire was the largest and most powerful the world had ever seen. London was its brain and brawn. In testament to its important status, London hosted the international Great Exhibition in 1851 at the Crystal Palace. A tribute to industrialism, the grand show was held in a specially designed glass building featuring the splendors and riches of the monarchy and the United Kingdom.

Londoners benefited from the ripple effects of industrialization and colonial power in the nineteenth century, as blue-collar wages doubled and the standard of living improved. The city undertook major sanitation infrastructure projects, and new sewer and clean drinking water systems were commissioned. These were instrumental in lowering the city's death rate as they dramatically reduced the spread of disease. These measures also cleared up the Thames, which had become so filthy that the summer of 1848 was called the "Great Stink."

Above: Statue of Sir Winston Leonard Spencer-Churchill at Parliament Square, looking towards Westminster Palace. Churchill, England's Prime Minister from 1940 to 1945 and from 1951 to 1955, marked the city in difficult times. He was one of history's greatest men.

London's good fortune derailed in the twentieth century, as it became an important target during World Wars I and II. Over twenty thousand Londoners were killed during the Blitz of 1940-41, and many old buildings were destroyed.

London rebuilt again, and the British Empire dwindled as colonies sought independence and the kingdom's coffers were depleted. But a new era in world dominance began: popular culture. Along with the Mod fashion of the 1950s and '60s came The Kinks and The Who, then the spirit of the 1960s brought love, peace, and The Beatles. Later, it was The Rolling Stones, and in the 1970s, the Sex Pistols. Young people the world over waited to see what would come out of London next; fashion, music, and trends kept the city on the front pages. It was *the* place to be. London remains one of the top cities in the world for fashion and music.

Above: Old and modern London: the Tower of London and 30 St. Mary Axe, known by many as "The Gherkin."
Right: Westminster Palace, seat of Parliament of the United Kingdom.

Today, London stands for many things. London is loved for its history of kings and queens, for its elegance and grit. Even if Prince Charles says he does not love the architecture, millions of others love such old London landmarks as Westminster Palace, and the new ones as well, such as the Millennium Wheel.

London stands for multiculturalism, since the city is home to over 7.5 million people, many of them from beyond the island. Visitors who pass through Heathrow International Airport can never forget the experience of the world's busiest airport. London stands for diversity and excitement: writers and poets, artists and musicians leave their traces in the city's distinctive neighborhoods—Knightsbridge, Chelsea, Kensington, Paddington, Notting Hill, to name a few.

When foreigners think of London they think of the Tube, black taxi cabs, and double-decker buses. They think of Britpop music, the sky-piercing building at 30 St. Mary Axe, also known as the Gherkin, and "bobbies" who police the streets with no firearms in their belts. And at risk of peril, every tourist from outside the UK and its former colonies should always, always be thinking about how Londoners drive on the left side of the street.

We love the fascinating royal history of London and the way the city remains a reference point for English culture around the world today.

"You find no man, at all intellectual, who is willing to leave London. No, Sir, when a man is tired of London, he is tired of life; for there is in London all that life can afford."
—*Writer Samuel Johnson*

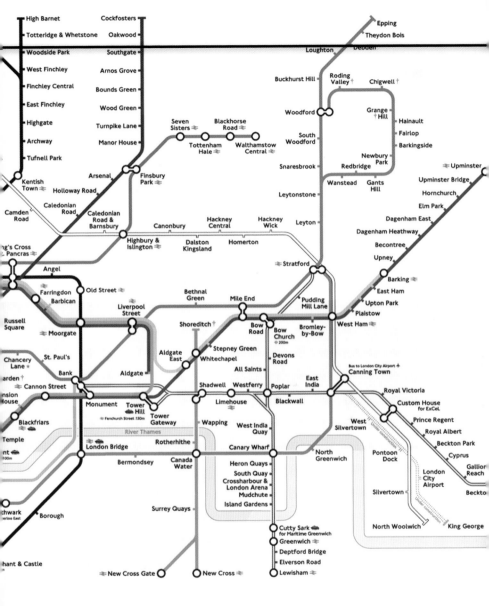

Above: London's underground transit system, also known simply as "The Tube". It opened in 1863, and was the first underground railway system in the world. Used as a shelter during World War II, the transit system saved many lives. Currently, some three million people use it every day.

Patrick Bonneville: One has to have walked the streets of Tokyo to understand its grandeur. This city seems to never end and has many layers. The hearts of Tokyo beat healthy, young, and fast.

Tokyo Metropolis sits in an unlucky region, where it is at the mercy of the environment and Mother Nature. Tokyo has risen phoenix-like from the ashes of volcanoes, earthquakes, and devastating fires, but to its credit, these disadvantages have been mere catalysts for persistence and progress. Records show that between 1600 and 1945, the city was destroyed every twenty-five to fifty years by fires, earthquakes, tsunami, volcanoes or war.

The seeds of modern Tokyo grew at the heart of a fishing village known as Edo. Chosen specifically for its canals, the shogun Tokugawa Ieyasu built the area into a strong military and government center in the late sixteenth century. By the early 1700s the population was well into the millions; Edo was the most populous city in the world at that time. The feudal regime of the Tokugawa Shogunate, or *bakufu* period, lasted until 1867, when the last shogun was challenged to resign by the emperor. Edo was renamed Tokyo, which means "eastern capital," and the city officially became the administrative center of Japan.

Under the reign of Emperor Meiji, who ruled until 1912, Tokyo grew like a Western city. In striking contrast to the traditional wooden structures typical of a Japanese urbanscape, the era was

Above: Tokyo's *honbasho* (Grand Sumo Tournament
Right: Man playing *taiko*, Japanese "wide drum".

marked by an increasing use of concrete and brick. Roads were paved with stone, steam trains began to serve the people, and in 1869 the first telecommunications line was opened. The legacy of the Meiji Emperor was the placing of Tokyo at the forefront of technology and civilization, which is why the period is now known as the Meiji Restoration or Renewal.

When U.S. Navy Commodore Matthew Perry landed in Edo in 1853 to seek a trade agreement with Japan, Meiji was intrigued. With Perry, he effectively opened Japan to the West and combined Western advancements in technology and industry with Eastern values. Tokyo, and by extension Japan, successfully carved a permanent seat in the arena of world affairs.

Upon the death of the Emperor in 1912, a new era emerged. Not unlike other city centers of the world that experienced urban migration, citizens moved to Tokyo to work, spend, learn and play. Girls and women were given educational opportunities that made them the envy of their American and British counterparts.

Disaster struck in September 1923, when the Great Kanto Earthquake leveled the city to the ground, killing over 140,000 people. This mother of quakes—a whopping 8.3 on the Richter scale—caused the 93-ton Great Buddha statue at Kamakura to slide forward some two feet. The quake, its aftershocks, resulting fires and a typhoon made slivers of the city's wooden structures, and left an estimated 1.9 million homeless.

The strength of Tokyo's citizens and architecture had been put to the test. The event brought Tokyo to the forefront of building design and construction, as planners studied the buildings that did not fall and developed earthquake-proof buildings and strict building codes. They constructed prototypes and tested the structures prior to construction; Tokyo still houses the largest of these testing sites. The city was rebuilt to include large public park areas that would serve as shelters in case of future earthquakes. Tokyo observes Disaster Prevention Day every September, and events are held annually to remember past victims and to prevent future disasters through practice drills. These reminders are crucial to the survival of its more than 12 million residents.

Tokyo's population had seen steady growth since the 1600s, but, sadly, war technology brought an end to that. The 1940s brought war to Japan, and with it, came bombs. Although Hiroshima and Nagasaki were subjected to severe bombing, Tokyo was bombed no less than a hundred times. By 1945, the population was only 3.49 million, half of what it had been five years earlier.

The 1964 Olympic Games came to Tokyo, which welcomed athletes and visitors on its newly created *shinkansen,* or "bullet trains." Reaching out from the capital to other city centers are multiple rail routes, on which high-speed trains connect travelers to their destinations at speeds up to 300 km/hour. Tokyo didn't stop advancing with the *shinkansen;* by the mid 1980s, the city was at the center of cutting-edge technology, information, culture, fashion, and public security.

Well-being	9/10
Historical role	7.5/10
Attraction	9/10
Population	10/10
Dynamism	10/10
Average score	9.1/10

Left: The Tokyo Tower located in Shiba Park. Standing at 332.5 metres (1,091 ft.), it is the tallest structure in Japan.
Below: The Greater Tokyo transit system is the world's most extensive, with its 13 lines and 282 stations.

Tokyo is a study in contradiction: you can be buffeted about by its movement and hyperactivity, but turn the corner and you find yourself in a Zen garden. Consult an oracle in the Shinto temple of Kannon, the city's oldest, join the bustle of the markets of Asakusa or shop in the electric shock of Akihabara. Tokyo is light and action. Tokyo is safety and environmental consciousness. Tokyo always surprises, delights, and evolves—as fast as the speed of light and as sure as the next earthquake.

We love the ultramodern beat of Tokyo that is wrapped up in an exquisite Asian aesthetic.

Tokyo ranks as a world class city because of its size and dynamism. It is the world's largest metropolitan economy and is home to some 35 million people, including its surrounding areas. The city thrives through its twenty-three central wards, each unique in character and each as important as the next. City dwellers work and play in the shadow of the wondrous and ever-present Mount Fuji, which gives the city an imposing allure.

Above: The Mode Gakuen Cocoon Tower. This 50-story building is home to a fashion school, a design college and a medical college.

Patrick Bonneville: The empire still breathes in its walls and vestiges. Rome was not built in a day, nor was it destroyed in a day. In the twenty-first century, The Eternal City is full of life, a proud testimony to modern urbanization. NYC is not the mother of all cities; Rome is. After all, all roads lead to Rome.

Had this book been written a few centuries ago, Rome would have held the number one spot. Known in its day as *Caput Mundi,* or the capital of the world, the city governed an enormous empire for four centuries, from about 44 BC to 476 AD. The colonies stretched as far north as modern-day England, south to North Africa, west, to Spain, and east, to Iran.

The legacy of ancient Rome is vast: the Empire left us the foundations of our art and culture and law and religion, those qualities that define, in part, the West today. Indeed, modern Rome is inexorably connected to its historic roots, for behind nearly every modern structure is a glimpse of its glorious past. The frequently appearing abbreviation SPQR on plaques in Rome is a reminder of those days; it stands for the Latin democratic motto *Senatus Populusque Romanus*, or "The Senate and People of Rome," the signature of the ancient government.

Rome's illustrious history dates to the eighth century BC, when it was established along an important trade route between the Etruscans in the north and the Greek colonies to the south. Classical legend has it that the twins Remus and Romulus, who were raised by a wolf, established the city. Romulus killed his brother and gave the new settlement his own name.

With a history so rich in culture and engineering technology and with a legacy of such tremendous political power, it is difficult to summarize the city's glories. For almost one thousand years, ancient Rome was the most important city in Europe. At its height, the city was the governing hub for the colonies garnered through Roman exploits and victories. The empire cast its net broadly in its search for riches and power, and dominated lands that included today's London, Paris, and Barcelona. Although Rome's importance in international affairs declined alongside the Roman Empire, its role as the seat of religious command continued. The rulers became popes and Rome became the Holy City.

Right: *The Death of Caesar*, by Jean-Léon Gérôme (1867). The painting depicts the assassination of Octavius, the first emperor of the Roman Empire, on March 15 in 44 BC.

"I found Rome brick, I left it marble."
—Augustus Caesar

For another significant era, we move forward to the fifteenth century, when Pope Sixtus IV spent many resources to improve the city. A civic patron of Rome, his efforts heralded in a new and glorious time. He built churches, including the Sistine Chapel, and public squares and bridges. He restored the aqueducts, which brought improvements in public health, and restored more than thirty churches. He encouraged music and painting and instigated a reform in the Julian calendar. He is responsible for refurbishing the Vatican Library and granting bishops the right to donate the bodies of executed criminals to science; from them, anatomist Vesalius and his students were able to compile the revolutionary medical anatomy text, *De humani corporis fabrica.*

The fifteenth century also brought us the works of Michelangelo, Perugino, Raphael, Ghirlandaio, Luca Signorelli, Botticelli, and Cosimo Rosselli. These artists would literally color the walls, halls, and ceilings of churches and public buildings throughout the city. Five hundred years later, much is being done in Rome to preserve their contributions for all of humanity to relish.

Today Rome is the capital of Italy and the home of Vatican City, which is the center of the Roman Catholic Church. Rome is Italy's largest metropolis, with over 3.7 million people in the metropolitan area. The city was untouched during World War II and so has retained its ancient ruins and Renaissance and Baroque flavor. As the third most popular tourist destination in Europe, many would probably agree that the city center deserves its UNESCO designation as a World Heritage Site.

Indeed, a touristic stroll through the center of Rome today is a journey back in time and culture. Cobble-stoned streets, and old—even ancient—buildings are reminders of greatness. Rome captures curiosity and peaks the senses. Visitors might make a pilgrimage of the religious or touristic kind to Vatican City. There, they might wander about St. Peter's Basilica, or the Apostolic Palace, or countless other churches. For a taste of the Renaissance, visitors and Romans alike marvel at the architecture and ornamentation of the Piazza del Campidoglio, the Palazzo Senatorio, the Palazzo Venezia, and other public places. The must-see stops on a tourist itinerary, however, are the ruins of the great Empire. Its famous landmarks include the Colosseum, the Roman Forum, the Pantheon, the Catacombs, the Circus Maximus, and many others.

Romans are proud of their past and are equally proud of their present. Many consider their city to be the capital of elegant style, where sensuality vibrates loudly. Rome might also be considered the capital of the "Slow Food" movement and home cooking. Sapienza University has been enriching the lives of students since 1303, and art, music, and science are alive and well in the city today.

"While stands the Coliseum, Rome shall stand. When falls the Coliseum, Rome shall fall. And when Rome falls - the World."
—Lord Byron

Above: The Monumento Nazionale a Vittorio Emanuele II, also known as the *Altare della Patria* or *Il Vittoriano*. This monument honors Victor Emmanuel, the first king of unified Italy.
Right: The Vatican City and Holy See, a sovereign 44-acre state landlocked in Rome. It is the episcopal see of the Pope and of the world's more than one billion Catholics.

The Treaties of Rome were signed here in 1957. It seems eminently fitting that the treaty to establish the European Economic Community was signed in the city that has left echoes of its greatness throughout the European landscape.

We love this sensual city with its motor scooters, public kisses, and mouth-watering cuisine. And we love the way Rome never lets us forget its ancient grandeur.

Well-being	9/10
Historical role	10/10
Attraction	10/10
Population	7/10
Dynamism	7/10
Average score	8.6/10

Patrick Bonneville: Hong Kong is like a machine that supplies the whole world. Western and Eastern enterprises meet here. It doesn't matter if the city belongs to the United Kingdom or China; the city is going full speed and nothing can stop it.

Hong Kong is the New York of the other side of the world. Culture, finance, education, and dynamism; this city has it all. The main difference is demographic: Hong Kong is relatively homogenous, as most of its citizens are of Chinese descent.

Officially named Hong Kong Special Administrative Region, the city is a territory of the People's Republic of China. With its population of seven million people in a space of 407 square miles (1,054 km²), it is one of the most densely populated cities in the world.

The city became a Crown colony of the United Kingdom in 1842 and remained a dependent territory until its transfer back to the People's Republic of China in 1997. Under Chinese rule, it has retained some of its British-era features, such as its currency, legal and political systems, immigration control, transportation systems, and other aspects of lifestyle. The city looks to China for foreign affairs and defense.

Hong Kong is a crucial worldwide economic center and is often cited as the most liberal capitalist economy in the world. It has the world's sixth highest GDP per capita and supports 33 percent of the foreign capital coming into China. Since its return to China, it has remained one of the most powerful cities in the world and is now an important asset to China. Citizens enjoy special privileges, thanks to their British roots.

Hong Kong is renowned for its expansive skyline, which is a true reflection of its cosmopolitan personality. The city counts about 7,650 skyscrapers. The reason for this upward growth is that ground space is limited; the only way to build is up. There are more people living above the fourteenth floor in Hong Kong than in any other city on Earth. Hong Kong is practically vertical!

Above: Hong Kong and Chinese flags.
Right: The International Finance Centre. Completed in 2003, it is the tallest building in Hong Kong. More than 3,500 workers contributed to the construction of this 88-story building.

"The story of this great city is about the years before this night and the years of success that will surely follow it."
—The last British Hong Kong governor Chris Patten, June 30, 1997

We love Hong Kong for its uniqueness among world cities. If one city could prove that different philosophies can work together, Hong Kong is it. While the bulk of the population is Chinese, the cultural influences are remarkably Western. The city has two official languages: Chinese and English, and some city dwellers are trilingual, meaning they speak Cantonese, Putonghua, and English. This distinct atmosphere infuses its cinema, music, cuisine, and traditions.

We love Hong Kong for Victoria Peak. As visitors travel to its top on the Peak Tram, they pass the myriad of high-rises. The ride is so steep that the buildings appear to be leaning at a 45° angle! Visible from the top are the world-famous skyline, the spectacular Victoria Harbour, and the serene green hillside.

We love the public transit system that carries over eleven million passengers a day. It includes two high-capacity railways, trams, buses, minibuses, taxis, and ferries. There are about 275 licensed vehicles for every one kilometer of roadway. About 90 percent of travel in the city is on public transportation, the highest rate in the world.

We simply love that Hong Kong integrates the best of two worlds—the exotic life of Imperial China and the liberty of Great Britain. It is a city of contrasts, contradictions, and equilibrium. We love that you can take Hong Kong out of Britain, but you can't take Britain out of Hong Kong!

Background: Statue of the famous Hong Kong actor Bruce Lee.
Below: Ferry crossing Victoria Harbour.
Right: The dragon is a strong symbol in Hong Kong culture. It is used as the official brand to promote the city worldwide.

Well-being	7.5/10
Historical role	6.5/10
Attraction	9.5/10
Population	10/10
Dynamism	9/10
Average score	8.5/10

"The Soviet Union has no moral or political right to interfere in the affairs of its East European neighbors. They have the right to decide their own fate."
—Mikhail Gorbachev, October 1989

Patrick Bonneville: In 1989, the city started to breathe again. The iron curtain fell and a beautiful, warm city emerged from five decades of darkness.

Today's Berlin is a diverse metropolis of 3.4 million, 5 million including surrounding areas. It is the capital of Germany as well as its largest city. Over 190 nationalities enrich its neighborhoods.

Berlin was founded in the thirteenth century, although the region it occupies has graced history books since at least the first century AD, when Germanic tribes controlled the area outside the Roman Empire's borders.

The later history of Berlin is tied to the history and greatness of Prussia during the eighteenth and nineteenth centuries. Prussia exerted great influence over much of northern Europe, until its demise under Adolf Hitler's Nazi Germany.

World War I hit Berlin hard. With over 2.5 million people in the city and surrounding areas to be fed, many suffered. After the war, the city was left poor and in dire need of a leader, and strikes and angry protests filled the streets of Berlin. From this void, Hitler rose to power, and by 1933 his party had ended democracy and begun the rule of nationalist socialism in Berlin and Germany.

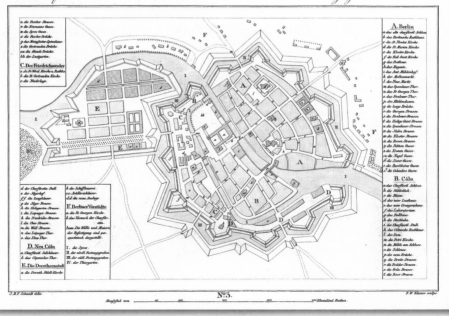

During World War II, Berlin became center stage for this party built on prejudice and intimidation. The eyes of the world were fixed on the city and anxiety and terror filled its streets. In January 1945, the Soviet Union's Red Army engaged Hitler in the Battle for Berlin. It ended with Hitler's suicide on April 30 and the surrender of the city on May 2. The city was all but annihilated: 600,000 apartments were destroyed, and only half of the city's population remained.

In accordance with an agreement signed by the Allies, Berlin was divided into four sectors, one each to be governed by the United States, France, Great Britain, and the Soviet Union. A great exodus from the Soviet-controlled east part of the city, between 1945 and 1961, caused a severe drop in population for East Berlin. The Soviets took the problem in hand by raising, on August 13, 1961, a temporary barrier to separate East Berlin from West Berlin. Roads connecting the two halves were ripped up, and guards were posted there.

The permanent wall that was soon constructed was 43.1 kilometers long. The border fortifications that separated West Berlin from the rest of the Soviet-controlled German Democratic Republic were 111.9 kilometers long. Over 100,000 people tried to escape East Berlin, and many of them were shot and killed by border guards.

Left: Map of Berlin from 1688. The 17th century attracted people from all over Europe to Berlin, from places like France, Bohemia and Austria.
Following page: The Brandenburg Gate, an important historical symbol of Berlin and Germany.

Life continued in this fashion for some twenty-five years, until Soviet President Mikhail Gorbachev indicated that he did not support the hard-line positions of the East German regime. In 1987, then U.S. President Ronald Reagan visited West Berlin and addressed the public with his famous "Mr. Gorbachev, tear down this wall!" speech. Indeed, the wall fell after a series of demonstrations and calls from international heads of government, beginning on November 9, 1989. Complete reunification was officially proclaimed on October 3, 1990.

Today, Berlin is a European center for contemporary art and music. It is home to more than four hundred art galleries, as well as zoos, botanical gardens, and important broadcast and print media companies. Berlin has been the city of choice for decades for artists seeking inspiration, innovation, and support.

We love Berliners for their tenacity and courage in resisting Hitler and his regime. We love Berliners for their life-risking attempts to tunnel under, fly over, and climb the Berlin Wall to see their friends and families on the other side. We love the city for its support of the arts and its continued presence on the world stage and for its universities and high tech industries. We love Berlin for the hope and peace it brought to the world when the Wall came down.

Well-being	8/10
Historical role	10/10
Attraction	7.5/10
Population	9/10
Dynamism	7.5/10
Average score	8.4/10

"Eventually, I think Chicago will be the most beautiful great city left in the world."
—Frank Lloyd Wright

"My first day in Chicago, September 4, 1983. I set foot in this city, and just walking down the street, it was like roots, like the motherland. I knew I belonged here."
—Oprah Winfrey

The area that is Chicago today was settled in the 1770s and was incorporated as a town in 1833, with a population of 350 people. The current city population stands at roughly 9.8 million including the metropolitan region.

Known as the "Windy City," Chicago nevertheless records average wind speeds that are lower than other U.S. cities, such as Boston and New York City. The city might be particularly windy because of how the wind scoops down the grid-built streets as if they were wind tunnels. Others might say the nickname has stuck because of the city's politicians!

The area was the site of many wars with local Native Americans, since it was a prized spot between the Great Lakes and the Mississippi River watershed. Original settlers were the Algonquian, Mascouten, and Miami peoples. The first non-native permanent settler in Chicago was Jean Baptiste Pointe du Sable, a Haitian, who married a local Potawatomi woman named Kittahawa. He is known as the Father of Chicago and was officially declared the city's founder by the State of Illinois and the City of Chicago on October 26, 1968. Du Sable's history is a remarkable one: a free black man in an era of slavery and intimidation, his entrepreneurial talents augmented his intelligence and enthusiasm. When he opened the first fur trading post in Chicago, he led the way for other Chicago dreamers to dare.

Native Americans ceded the land to the United States in 1816 with the Treaty of St. Louis. The next big step for the town was the opening of the Illinois and Michigan Canal in 1848. Shipping from the Great Lakes through to the Mississippi River down to the Gulf of Mexico was now possible. Chicago was an important stop on this route, and the city reaped the economic benefits. The first rail line into the city, the Galena & Chicago Union Railroad, was opened the same year. Chicago's role along the travel routes of the world hasn't diminished: today, Chicago's O'Hare International Airport is the second busiest airport in the world.

Well-being	8.5/10
Historical role	7.5/10
Attraction	8.5/10
Population	8.5/10
Dynamism	8.5/10
Average score	8.3/10

Right: American President Barack Obama grew as a world political figure in the city and state he first served, Chicago, Illinois. His permanent private residence is still in Chicago.

With ease of transport and shipping came big retail names. Montgomery Ward and Sears, Roebuck and Company set up catalogue shopping with their home bases in Chicago. The city grew quickly: in 1840, it was the ninetieth most populous city in the United States, and by 1842, it had moved to ninth place.

The city recovered from the Great Chicago Fire of 1871 in time for the World's Columbian Exposition, more famously known as The Chicago World's Fair, in 1893. It was timed to celebrate Christopher Columbus' arrival in the New World. Chicago had beaten rival cities New York, Washington D.C., and St. Louis to the honor of hosting the fair. The event was a great showcase and boosted Chicago's reputation as a city of architecture, art, and industrialism.

Its reputation attracted waves of people to the city, including a large number of African Americans. The population explosion created social tensions due to limited housing and jobs, which led to the Chicago Race Riot of 1919. For about a week, rioters swarmed the streets in a rage of murder and violence. Dozens were killed and hundreds were injured. Of the twenty-five riots that occurred that summer across the country, this was the worst. The period is now known as the Red Summer of 1919.

Chicago also attracted many "undesirables." Gangsters secretly controlled a good deal of the city's industry and wealth. Al Capone, the notoriously violent gangster, had a personal empire worth $108 million in 1927—the average annual American salary at that time was about $1,000 per year.

We love Chicago for many reasons. We love that Harold Washington was elected the first black mayor of Chicago in 1983. We love that Chicago is the home of the current U.S. President, Barack Obama. We love that the city attracts over thirty-two million domestic visitors and over one million foreign visitors every year. We love Chicago's skyscrapers. We love the empire Oprah Winfrey has built in this city. We love the sports teams of Chicago: the Cubs, the White Sox, the Bears, the Bulls, the Black Hawks. We love that Chicago has always been a city that encouraged the American Dream, for everybody. We love it that Chicago has always prized equality for immigrants and African Americans— even when it was unpopular to do so.

Patrick Bonneville: The city might not have the charm or the heritage of other major Chinese cities, but this metropolis is fueled by a very strong economic drive. Shanghai is growing at full speed.

Kimberly Murray: I was in Shanghai during China's national holiday week in October 2007. The city was inundated with tourists from around the country. I read that the city's population of 20 million people was expected to double that week. The pollution and lack of cleanliness bothered me, but the best memory I have is walking along the boardwalk at sunrise. Couples were dancing, others were practicing tai chi, and a stranger asked me to be in a picture with her!

Shanghai is the largest city in China. With over 20 million inhabitants, it is one of the largest metropolitan areas in the world. Officially, its name means "the upper reaches of the sea."

Shanghai was a sleepy fishing and textiles town until the nineteenth century. In 1842, following the Treaty of Nanking, Shanghai was established as a port town and opened to foreign trade and foreign influence. For a time, the city was notorious for its illegal opium trade. During the Japanese occupation of the 1930s and '40s, some 149 "comfort houses" were established in Shanghai, where Korean sex slaves were treated brutally and kept available for Japanese soldiers night and day.

With the rise to power of Mao Zedong's Communist government, foreign investment stopped and the city's economy remained in stasis. Shanghai revived during the 1990s when economic reforms were introduced and increased investments were allowed from both international and domestic investors. By 2005 Shanghai had became the world's largest cargo port, and since 1992, the city's annual growth has fluctuated between 9 and 15 percent. Although Shanghai occupies only 0.1 percent of China's land surface, it manages about 25 percent of the country's port trade.

An important area of development is the Pudong zone, which sits on the opposite side of the Huangpu River, across from the traditional neighborhoods of Shanghai. The Pudong skyline of high-rises, including especially the Oriental Pearl Tower, is remarkably different than that of the Bund, Shanghai's older neighborhood. The sector known as the French Concession was cosmopolitan in flavor until the Mao regime and his Cultural Revolution, and its buildings, architecture, and street layout reveal a strong European influence.

Left: Shanghai's famous landmark, The Oriental Pearl.
Above: Skyline of one of the fastest growing cities.

Within China, the city enjoys a reputation of modernism. It is the city of choice for many Chinese at vacation time. The first motorcar in China was driven in Shanghai, and it was also the first city to be fitted with a modern sewage system. Especially before the Cultural Revolution, Shanghai drew the attention of many writers and intellectuals, as the East-meets-West atmosphere fed their imagination and encouraged forward thinking. Shanghai is also the center of cinema and theater in modern-day China.

We don't love the lack of sufficient housing for citizens, or the quality of the air, or the lack of street cleanliness in Shangai. The city is faced with a considerable air pollution challenge due to its use of coal energy in industry and for heating homes. Its waterways are severely polluted as well, and Shanghai has undertaken a $1 billion project to clean the Suzhou Creek. We do love that the city's organic waste is transported to rural areas to be used as fertilizer and that its solid waste is used for landfill or brick-making.

Left: The very busy Nanjing Street.
Above: Building new skyscrapers near the Shanghai World Financial Center.
Right: Green oasis in the middle of the city.

While the media façade of Shanghai today is that of a prototypical modern Chinese city, down the narrow cobblestone roads lies the ancient Shanghai, with its temples and parks, men playing Mahjong, and kids throwing balls. We love that juxtaposition of time and culture. We love that Shangai is a city in constant evolution with no plans to slow down.

Well-being	6/10
Historical role	7/10
Attraction	8/10
Population	10/10
Dynamism	10/10
Average score	8.2/10

Patrick Bonneville: Vienna is the heart of the Continent - where Eastern and Western Europe meet.

Vienna conjures images of music and artists and history and grandeur. It is the capital of the Republic of Austria and one of its nine states. Vienna has a population of about 1.7 million, or 2.3 million in the whole metropolitan area. In 2005, an Economist Intelligence Unit study of 127 world cities ranked it first, in a tie with Vancouver, for quality of life. The Mercer Survey mirrored this assessment in 2009.

Vienna's history begins with a supposed Celtic settlement called Vindobona, prior to the arrival of the Romans in the first century AD. Later, the city grew rapidly due to trade, and by the eleventh century was an important hub for cross-European commerce. Eventually, Vienna became the capital of the Holy Roman Empire, and in the sixteenth and seventeenth centuries it was a cultural center for musicians, artists, scientists, and even for chefs! The city protected its freedom fiercely, and stopped two invasions by the Ottoman empire, in 1529 at the Siege of Vienna and in 1683, in the Battle of Vienna.

With time, the city sprawled, and by the early 1900s the population stood at close to two million. The 1920s introduced "Red Vienna" to the world, as the city experimented with socialism and rebellion. In 1938, when the Nazis occupied Vienna, Hitler divested the city of its status as capital and Austrians were subject to government from Berlin. Near the end of World War II,

Vienna was freed from the Germans in the Vienna Offensive, when the Soviets besieged the city for nearly two weeks. Vienna was then divided into four zones and was governed by the Allied Commission for Austria. Once again the capital of Austria, the city remained under foreign occupation for ten years.

Despite its political history, which is laced with war and exploitation, Vienna is a city of masquerade balls, choirs—including the famous Vienna Boys' Choir—and great concert halls. It remains to this day the leader in modern day gala balls, with over two hundred significant events held every year in its beautiful halls, such as the Hofburg Palace at Heldenplatz. There are classic balls, such as the formal Opera Ball, but also local events that are jovial and popular with all classes of people.

We love Vienna for being an important European educational center with no fewer than eighteen universities. We love that the city has the world's oldest zoo, The Tiergarten Schönbrunn. We love Viennese architecture, castles, and Old-World-charm cafés, like the Café Hawalka. We love that the city center was designated a UNESCO World Heritage Site in 2001. We love Vienna for how it has nurtured, inspired, and encouraged music and high culture, from the earliest days of its existence to today.

Left: Schönbrunn Palace Gardens, former residence of the Habsburg monarchs, including Franz Joseph I and his beloved wife Elisabeth "Sissi" of Bavaria. Schönbrunn means "beautiful spring".
Above: The Rathaus, Vienna's city hall, in the Christmas season.
Right: Statue of Johann Strauss II. Strauss was known as "The Waltz King" of Vienna. He died in Vienna in 1899.

Well-being	10/10
Historical role	8/10
Attraction	8.5/10
Population	7.5/10
Dynamism	7/10
Average score	8.2/10

Kim Murray: I traveled to Beijing in the fall of 2007. Beijing surprised me. From its quaint alleys and grand thoroughfares to its sheer size and understated elegance, it is a city that radiates from within.

Beijing, whose name means "northern capital," is the capital city of the People's Republic of China. It has a population of about 17 million and is recognized as the political, educational, and cultural center of the country.

Fossils of *homo erectus* that date back 250,000 years have been found in the Fangshan District—those 1920s discoveries brought us Peking Man. Cities are known to have been in the area by 1,000 BC and Ji, the capital city of the state of Yan, was established in present-day Beijing in 473 BC.

The city has been known by many names throughout history, including Zhongdu, Beiping, and Peking. It was believed to have been the largest city of the world from 1425 to 1650 and again from 1710 to 1825. Beijing's long and royal history brought us the Imperial Palace, Summer Palace, Winter Palace, Tiananmen Square, and other great halls and monuments.

The twentieth century blew a wind of change across China. Mao Zedong declared the creation of the People's Republic of China in 1949, and the newly renamed Beijing was also reinstated as its capital. Chairman Mao used some of Beijing's ancient city walls, which he ordered deconstructed during the Cultural Revolution, to build an underground city that would protect him and 40 percent of the city's citizens in case of a nuclear attack by the USSR. The tunnels still exist, and some of them have been opened to the public.

The city is heavily polluted, but we do love that Beijing has taken significant steps toward reducing pollution. The city implemented a $17 billion project for air-improvement practices in time for its role as host of the 2008 Olympic Games. According to the United Nations Environmental Program, Beijing has also introduced 3,800 natural gas buses and has updated and expanded green spaces in an effort to make the city more livable and more green.

We love Beijing for opening the Forbidden City, now The Imperial Palace Museum, to visitors. It is also a UNESCO World Heritage Site. We love its various tourist attractions, including palaces and temples and, nearby, the Great Wall of China. And, finally, we love Beijing for its people, who greet foreigners with smiles and nods, and even with bows from the elderly and giggles from the children.

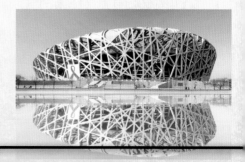

ft: The spectacular Beijing National Stadium, built for the 2008 Olympic Games.
low: Lion statue inside the Summer Palace. Guardian lion statues are strong protective symbols in Beijing.

Well-being	6/10
Historical role	9/10
Attraction	8/10
Population	9.5/10
Dynamism	8/10
Average score	8.1/10

Patrick Bonneville: Since its independence and thriving economic success, Singapore has fired a spark in the hearts of other cities that dream of a similar destiny.

Singapore is officially the Republic of Singapore, an island city-state on the southern tip of the Malay Peninsula, in Indonesia. It is a microstate and the smallest nation in Southeast Asia. It has a population of 5 million people, of whom 76.8 percent are of Chinese origin, 13.9 percent Malay, 7.9 percent Indian, and the rest composed of various groups.

This region was mapped as early as the second century AD. Written history speaks of the Mongol Yuan Dynasty sending a mission to the region to collect elephants in 1320. There is also an historical account of Chinese settlers on the island in 1330.

Temasek, "sea town," was the name given to an early version of Singapore, and it is still used by corporations and for national honors in the city. In 1613, Portuguese explorers burnt the town to the ground and it remained in the shadows for the next two hundred years. Britain finally established a port in Singapore in 1819, as the British were eager to protect their merchant fleets throughout the East Indies from the Dutch. Within three years of its foundation, the port was earning revenues that surpassed Britain's other port, Penang. In 1824, with the signing of the Anglo-Dutch Treaty, the Dutch withdrew all objections to the British occupation of Singapore.

More changes came when, in 1826, Singapore, Malacca, and Penang were grouped under the single administration of British India to form the Straits Settlements. Singapore was the chosen capital of this group and it wasn't long before the region would became a Crown colony under the control of the United Kingdom.

On August 9, 1965, Singapore separated from newly created Malaysia, to which it had been joined, to become a sovereign, democratic, and independent nation. The city-state was accepted at the United Nations on September 21, 1965, and to the Commonwealth of Nations on October 15, 1965. It would become a republic just two months later, on December 22, 1965.

Above: 75% of the population in Singapore is Chinese.

Well-being	8.5/10
Historical role	6.5/10
Attraction	8.5/10
Population	8/10
Dynamism	9/10
Average score	8.1/10

We love Singapore for its "American Dream" philosophy—with desire, ambition, know-how, and ability, anyone can set up shop in Singapore and be prosperous. Business and income taxes are relatively low and allow entrepreneurs a chance to get their companies off the ground. We love Singapore's attraction factor. About ten million people visit the city every year. According to the World Bank's annual World Development Report of 2009, Singapore is a perfect model of development and "effective urbanization." The city transformed its rural slums into "one of the cleanest and most welcoming cities in the world" in just forty years.

Above: Singapore skyline. The business and financial center is known as the Downtown Core.

We love that Singapore is a democracy under its current prime minister. It is also transparent in its business practices and in government, which makes it one of the world's ten most "free from corruption" countries. We love that Singapore is tough on crime, although we acknowledge that practices of corporal and capital punishment draw plenty of criticism. Last of all, we love Singapore's attractions. Between its 4,000-plus skyscrapers, crystal-clear waters, and multitude of sports and activities, Singapore is a haven for residents and a tourist's dream come true.

Patrick Bonneville: Barcelona has a soul as strong as any of the biggest cities of the world. Its animated residents and its eccentric architects have given the city a truly unique flavor.

Despite its small size, this city of trade and art deserves acknowledgement. Barcelona has a population of about 5 million including the suburbs, but only 1,603,178 in the city proper. But what marks this Catalonian city is its Mediterranean soul, which has seeped into local parks and beaches, and into the culture and languages.

As with many other European cities, Barcelona's roots reach back to the Roman Empire. In expanding its reach westward, Rome merged with the existing Kingdom of Aragon and established a colony at this Meditteranean port, located between Europe and North Africa. After the fall of Rome, Barcelona passed through the hands of the Visigoths, Moors, and Franks before becoming an independent county with strong links to Europe, while the counties surrounding it were linked with the Moors. The city was known by many names in its course through human history: in Latin as Barcino, and as Barcinona, Barcelo, Barceno, Barchinona, Barçalona, Barchelona and Barchenona.

Towards the end of the eighteenth century, an important discovery of lignite, a low-grade coal, was made in the area, and with that arrived wealth for the city. Barcelona hosted the Universal Exposition in 1888 and used the opportunity to expose its industrial advances and social power to the world. This exhibit would cement Barcelona's reputation as a cultural center.

The city's world-class status is confirmed today in the works of architect Antoni Gaudí (1852-1926). At the time, his work was ridiculed and he found little financial backing, yet Barcelona embraced his vision and his art. Gaudí created works that reflected nature, or rather, his observation of nature. His goal was to surround the city with buildings and parks that would evoke inspiration. Over one hundred years later his work still creates debate, although its value was confirmed when UNESCO conferred upon the architectural works of Gaudí and his colleague Lluís Domènech i Montaner status as World Heritage Sites.

In 1929, Barcelona hosted a second International Exhibition. In preparation for the event, the city inaugurated a subway system in 1924. It was now indeed a cosmopolitan city. War came to Barcelona in 1938 under the command of Italian dictator Benito Mussolini.

Left: The interior of Casa Batllo, designed by the great Barcelonian architect Antoni Gaudí.
Right: Exterior of Casa Batllo. Gaudí left his mark everywhere in Barcelona, making it a very special city.

In attacks aimed at the Catalan people, the city was bombed for three days; the civilian population was on the receiving end. Almost one year and thousands of deaths later, the Catalan people lost to the hands of the Nationalists. Under the rule of dictator General Franco, Barcelonians lost their autonomous rights as Barcelona and Catalonia and were forbidden to speak Catalan, their native tongue. The region fell into the dim background of Europe.

Franco's death in 1975 opened the door to fresh air and democracy. Barcelona demanded change through peaceful demonstrations, as millions gathered in the streets and called for Catalan autonomy. In 1977, partial independence was restored to the Autonomous Community of Catalonia.

"Everything comes from the great book of nature."
—Antonio Gaudí

Well-being	9/10
Historical role	7/10
Attraction	9/10
Population	7/10
Dynamism	8/10
Average score	8.0/10

Left: The still unfinished Temple Expiatori de la Sagrada Família. Started in 1882, Gaudí's master-work is expected to be completed in 2026.
Right: Entrance of Park Güell, another bold chef-d'oeuvre signed by Gaudí. The park was completed in 1914.

Barcelona enjoyed being at the center of the world's attention as it hosted the 1992 Olympic Games. It has also come to be known once again as an important business center and Mediterranean port. Today, Barcelona is a city full of humanitarian organizations that help with local issues as well as international concerns. When it comes to protecting and promoting the Romani people of Europe, furthering the education of the Catalan people, or providing assistance to international causes, Barcelona is an ideal location for any organization. Because it is a city with a history of war and oppression, today's citizens strive to ensure equality and opportunity. For this, and for all it offers, Barcelona is a top-100 city.

We love the Catalan pride and flavor that permeates Barcelona.

Patrick Bonneville: I first thought Kyoto, Kobe, and Osaka should be treated as three separate entries, but they are so tightly woven together that they really form one metropolitan region. Although each has its own characteristics and particularities, together they form the megalopolis called Keihanshin.

Japan's second-largest metropolitan area is Keihanshin, with a population of just over 18.5 million people. It comprises the cities of Osaka, Kobe, and Kyoto.

The history of the region dates back to at least the eighth century, when Emperor Kammu moved his headquarters there to escape Buddhist influence. Originally, the area was known as Uda, but it eventually became the city of Kyoto, which means "capital city." The city of Kobe grew in importance in the thirteenth century, when it was an important port city known as Hyōgo Port. At Osaka, historical accounts speak of the Emperor Kōtoku who built his palace in 645 AD at a place known as Naniwa-kyō.

Keihanshin is the oldest industrial region of Japan, as its three cities grew in importance in Japan's port and trade industries. It is neither an administrative nor a political entity, and each city has its own governing rights. Both Kyoto and Osaka hold historical importance as ancient cities of politics, agriculture, industry and culture. Osaka and Kyoto focused on the textile and porcelain industries, and Kobe concentrated on cement, steel, glass, and rubber.

World War II brought bombs and death to Kobe. On March 17, 1945, American B-29 bombers flooded the skies and killed 8,841 people. About one quarter of the city was destroyed and more than 650,000 people lost their homes; another half million homes were badly damaged. Osaka was also heavily bombed by the United States and lost more than ten thousand civilian residents. On March 18, 1975, the Kobe City Council passed an ordinance that banned ships carrying nuclear weapons from its port; Kobe's citizens had long pressured the city to adopt such sanctions. Kyoto was spared from bombing during the war and as a result several pre-war buildings, such as the *machiya,* traditional wooden town-houses, can still be found.

Well-being	9/10
Historical role	7/10
Attraction	7/10
Population	9/10
Dynamism	8/10
Average score	8.0/10

All three cities have a special place in Japanese life. We love Kyoto for the well-preserved Japanese culture that echoes in lost alleys and behind modern **facades**. We love Kyoto's two thousand Buddhist temples and Shinto shrines and its seemingly endless palaces, gardens, and unique architecture. We absolutely love Kyoto for its seventeen World Heritage Site properties, which date from the tenth to the nineteenth centuries. We love the city's role in the environmental accord called the Kyoto Protocol. We also love the Gekkeikan Brewery, the oldest sake brewer in the world. Founded by the Okura family in 1637, it was the official sake of Japan's Imperial Household for close to one hundred years and is one of the oldest family-operated businesses in the world.

We are inspired by Kobe's Ikuta Shrine. It is possibly one of the oldest in Japan, believed to have been founded by Empress Jingū sometime around 300 AD; it is miraculous that the shrine wasn't destroyed in the 1995 earthquake. We love Kobe's unassuming personality as a cosmopolitan port with an international flavor. Set within stunning mountain scenery, Kobe is a feast for all of the senses. We also love Kobe's beef—some of the best and most famous in all of Japan.

"I told him there was one city that they must not bomb without my permission and that was Kyoto."
—Henry L. Stimson, United States Secretary of War during World War II

Left: Himeji Castle, located in Himeji near Kobe.
Above: Temple near Kyoto.

It is said that the cows are massaged with sake and given beer to drink! We also love Kobe's mix of new and old Japan, especially with modern buildings like the Fish Dance restaurant by architect Frank Gehry.

We love the Osaka Aquarium, which displays marine life from the Pacific Rim waters. We also love the city's Shitennoji Temple, which dates back to 593 AD. It was built to enshrine Prince Shotoku, who embraced Buddhism at a time when Shinto was practiced by the majority. It is said that Prince Shotoku invented the culinary dish of sushi, so great was his love of seafood. We also love the pagoda-style Osaka Castle, which sits insouciantly beside the skyscrapers of the business center. Last but not least, we love the Osaka International Peace Center. The museum is a testimony to the horrors of World War II that were propagated by the Japanese in various parts of Asia.

Patrick Bonneville: The big town Down Under. Sydney is the city that welcomes everyone to the gigantic land of Australia. The quality of life in Sydney measures high; the economy is strong, and Sydney is cool, stable, and beautiful. If not for its isolation and short history, this could be a top ten city.

There is historical and archeological proof that the area surrounding Port Jackson, or Sydney Harbour, has been home to Aboriginal tribes for over 40,000 years. In 1770, British Captain James Cook explored the area and reported on what he called Botany Bay. Not long after, in 1788, Arthur Phillip struck a settlement at Sydney Cove under the British flag. Originally known as "New Albion," the name was later changed to honor the then British Home Secretary, Thomas Townshend, Lord Sydney.

Not unlike colonial experiments in North America, European settlement in Australia had a catastrophic impact on the Aboriginal people. Nearly 50 percent of the population of Sydney succumbed to the diseases brought by settlers, especially from smallpox.

A gold discovery in Bathurst, some 150 kilometers west of Sydney, sparked an important gold rush in 1851. Immigrants flooded the ports, and within twenty years, Sydney's population grew from 39,000 to over 200,000. Along with its growing population came improvements to the city's infrastructure. By the end of the nineteenth century, the city had developed efficient suburban mass transit systems; today, Sydney's modern transit system is among the best organized in the world.

When Sydney Harbor was attacked by the Imperial Japanese Navy during World War II, the entire country joined the Allied forces. Immediately following the war, Australia became a founding member of the United Nations. This was a boom time for Australia and for Sydney. In 1973, the landmark white sails of the Sydney Opera House were inaugurated, and in 2007, the five-theater hall was declared a UNESCO World Heritage Site.

Well-being	9/10
Historical role	6/10
Attraction	9/10
Population	8/10
Dynamism	8/10
Average score	8.0/10

ft: Downtown acces to Australia's largest city.
ove: Harbor view of Sydney and its famous Opera House.

Sydney is the largest city in Australia and the state capital of New South Wales. The city contributes approximately 25 percent to the country's total GDP. Multiculturalism is evident everywhere—the city's rail transit website offers navigation choices in eleven languages! Sydney is a popular tourist destination for domestic vacationers and international travelers alike. The website Forbes Traveler recently graded Sydney the second happiest city in the world!

Citizens are known for their pro-environmental perspective. Many of them worked hard in the 1970s to preserve from development The Rocks, a neighborhood of sandstone buildings that is the historical precinct of central Sydney and a busy pub scene by night.

We love Sydney for the natural beauty of its beaches and for its gentle weather. We love that Sydneysiders are sports lovers who often carry their surfboards on the subway. Millions around the world loved watching the 2000 Olympic Games in Sydney. We love the Sydney skyline, in which simple buildings sit comfortably among expressionist constructions. And we love Sydney as a portal to the Australian outback and the other hidden treasures this country has to offer.

" [Sydney is like] something grand, famous and preferably glittering left on the shores of history by Empire's receding tide . . . Not I think the best of the cities the British Empire created, not the most beautiful either, but the most hyperbolic, the youngest at heart, the shiniest."
—Writer Jan Morris, in 1992

Patrick Bonneville: This is the refined America. A city forged on freedom and education, Boston is the grand lady of the North.

Boston is unique among American cities. It feels like a small town, yet it has a population of 4.5 million people. And while we think of North American towns as young, Boston is older than Saint Petersburg. Puritan colonists from England founded their colony here on September 17, 1630, but archeological excavations point to Native life in the region dating back at least 5,000 years.

Education was important to the Puritans and it was not long before learning institutions were built, beginning with the Boston Latin School in 1635 and Harvard University, then known as New College, in 1636.

With its excellent harbor, Boston became the leading commercial center in the colonies. Both shipbuilding and shipping were vital industries here, and by the 1770s, Boston's prosperity led Britain to seek more control—in the guise of taxes—over their New England colonies. Bostonians were not happy, and the American Revolution fomented. The city saw several important battles in the larger fight, including the Boston Massacre, the Boston Tea Party, and the Siege of Boston.

"And it was from Boston that one in every six American families began their journey into the land of the free."
—Thomas Menino

As the United States was born through the revolution, Boston struggled. Shipping activities were halted during the Napoleonic Wars, and not long after, the War of 1812 hit the region hard. Trade slowed down, and although the city had developed a manufacturing sector, it still suffered economically. This changed when Boston became a center for arms manufacturing during the Second World War.

By the end of the war, Boston had regained its prosperity. The city's many academic institutions, now including the Massachusetts Institute of Technology, fostered the growth of a strong scientific community, and by the 1950s, the computer and high-tech industries were bringing professors and businesses to the region.

Left: Boston's downtown and historic district is concentrated on the shore of Boston Harbor, a natural estuary of the Atlantic Ocean.

Twelve million tourists per year enjoy the city's maritime heritage and its old neighborhoods, such as the Haymarket and the port of Boston. We love that Boston is one of the greatest education centers of the world. We love Boston's sports teams: the Red Sox, the Patriots, the Celtics, and the Bruins. We love Boston for being the "cradle of liberty" and for standing up to the British Empire. We love Boston for being the center of the movement to abolish slavery in the United States.

We love that Boston includes its surrounding suburbs in daily life and that Boston enjoys a favorable relationship with its bigger neighbor, New York City. We love Boston's stability and economic strength. And we love the Boston accent!

Above: One of the oldest cemeteries in America, King's Chapel Burying Ground on Tremont Street was founded in 1630, and was the city's first.

"Massachusetts has been the wheel within New England, and Boston the wheel within Massachusetts. Boston therefore is often called 'the hub of the world,' since it has been the source and fountain of the ideas that have reared and made America."
—Reverend F.B. Zinckle, in his book on the Civil War

Well-being	9.5/10
Historical role	7.5/10
Attraction	7/10
Population	7.5/10
Dynamism	8/10
Average score	7.9/10

THE CITY OF PETER THE GREAT

Patrick Bonneville: Saint Petersburg is the soul of Russia. It is one of the most magnificent Northern European cities and its people have shaped the history of Russia. The city was a man's idea, but it was built and perfected by women with very good taste.

Founded by Tsar Peter I of Russia on May 27, 1703, Saint Petersburg was the heart of the Russian Empire for over two hundred years. Today this cultural capital is Russia's second most populous city, with over six million citizens in metropolitan and surrounding areas. The Historic Centre of Saint Petersburg and Related Groups of Monuments constitutes a UNESCO World Heritage Site.

Peter I, or Peter the Great, was educated in Amsterdam. As an adult, his vision was simple—open up a transportation route between Russia and Europe. He chose the shortest route possible, along the Neva River to the Baltic Sea. When this was achieved, Saint Petersburg was founded.

After Peter's death, his wife Catherine assumed the throne. She, in turn, passed on the role of monarch to her son Peter II and then to Peter the Great's daughter, Elizabeth. Elizabeth loved beauty, and under her leadership Saint Petersburg was endowed with luxury and comfort. Her nephew, Peter III, then took the throne but was overthrown by his wife. Catherine the Great continued in Elizabeth's shoes and turned Saint Petersburg into a grand city.

Catherine wished to be surrounded by a luxurious court and chose the newly built Winter Palace as her home. There, she initiated an impressive imperial collection of art, which is now the world-famous State Hermitage Museum. The Hermitage Theater was built close to her palace and was surrounded by new houses and mansions of the finest quality. Under her rule, the left embankments of the Neva River were lined with red granite, and intricate wrought iron fence-works were commissioned for the Summer Gardens.

Revolutions and mini-wars spanned the eighteenth and nineteenth centuries and led Emperor Nicholas I to push for Russian nationalism. Serfs were emancipated and tenement housing developments built for them on the outskirts of Saint Petersburg. Under the efforts of Tsar Alexander II, industrialization came to the city, and by 1900 it was the fourth largest in Europe and a major player on the international business and political scenes.

During World War I, Saint Petersburg was deemed too German a name to keep, and the city was renamed Petrograd. As the war raged, the Russian Revolution brewed, and not long after came the re-emergence of the Communist Party, led by Vladimir Lenin. Tsar Nicholas II was arrested, and a battle for communism and democracy began. Lenin moved the capital to Moscow on March 5, 1918. Initially intended as a temporary home in order to escape anti-Soviet forces, Moscow is still the

capital some ninety years later. Three days following his death, on January 24, 1924, Petrograd was baptized Leningrad in honor of this hero of the revolution.

Leningrad suffered during this period in its history. Crime and vandalism flourished during the revolutions and the wars, and in under two decades, two million people left the city for elsewhere in Russia, Europe, or America. The city was further devastated when World War II brought in Hitler's armies, who killed an estimated one million civilians. Buildings were destroyed by the dozens, and starvation, illness, and disease scoured the streets for victims. Those who stayed fought for their town and in 1945, the former USSR granted Leningrad the title of "Hero City."

Hidden between revolution and Soviet Communism, the great city was waiting to be reborn. That day came, when on September 6, 1991, a referendum was held to restore the prestigious name of Saint Petersburg. There was also a promise to ensure that revenues generated in Saint Petersburg would stay there.

Today, Saint Petersburg is a low-rise city; at first glance it seems unchanged from a hundred years ago. Controversial building projects are planned that could change that, however, and in 2008, the World Monuments Fund listed this historic skyline as one of the most endangered sites due to expansion.

We love Saint Petersburg for the courage of its citizens—from its humble beginnings, through the brutalities of the Second World War, and then under Soviet Communism. We love Saint Petersburg's museums: The Hermitage and also the museum-homes of Alexander Pushkin, Fyodor Dostoevsky, Nikolai Rimsky-Korsakov, Feodor Chaliapin, Alexander Blok, Vladimir Nabokov, Anna Akhmatova, Mikhail Zoshchenko, and Joseph Brodsky.

We love St. Isaac's Cathedral, and the city's gardens, and its skyscraper-free skyline. We love the city's famous port, canals, and waterways. We love that Alfred Nobel, of the Nobel Prize, spent many of his formative years in Saint Petersburg with his family. We love the bridges crisscrossing the Neva. We love the White Nights, in the last ten days of June, when the sun shines throughout the longest days of the year. And finally, we love that the citizens of Saint Petersburg gave it back its name.

"The Führer is determined to eliminate city of Petersburg from the face of eart There is no reason whatsoever for subs quent existence of this large-scale city the neutralization of the Soviet Russia."
—Nazi secret instruction, Sept. 23, 194

Well-being	7/10
Historical role	10/10
Attraction	8/10
Population	7.5/10
Dynamism	7/10
Average score	7.9/10

"The City of Banks" is more commonly known as Frankfurt. It has a population of nearly 700,000 in the city itself, and over 5.5 million in the metropolitan region.

The first mention of the name Frankfurt was found in a document belonging to Charlemagne. During its earlier history, however, the region served as a Roman military camp, the court of Franconian kings, and, from 1356 onwards, as an important city for the Holy Roman Empire. After the Franco-Prussian War ended in 1871, the city was absorbed by Prussia. The stock exchange, the Old Opera, and the central train station were constructed by the late 1800s, and the university and the first airport in the early 1900s.

Frankfurt was destroyed to a great extent by World War II Allied bombing, and its medieval appearances were rebuilt in a modern guise. About nine thousand Jews were deported from the city during the war and all synagogues in the city were destroyed. Today, there are about 7,300 Jews living in Frankfurt. After the war, the city narrowly lost out on its bid to be the country's capital, although it did go on to become an important business center. In 1998, Frankfurt became the seat of the European Central Bank.

Frankfurt is the largest financial center in continental Europe. It is the site of several large commercial banks: there are at least 228 credit institution headquarters in Frankfurt that, including the insurance industry, employ 70,560 people. The city is a favorite choice in the world for trade fairs, including for the Frankfurt Book Fair, the world's largest book show, and the Internationale Automobil-Ausstellung, the world's biggest car show.

Frankfurt is the only city in Germany with a large number of skyscrapers; most of them house banks and offices. During the workweek, the population explodes: there are nearly 600,000 jobs in the city—almost as many employees as the actual population. They come on the autobahn highway or on public transportation, including underground trains, trams, and buses. The Frankfurt airport is the second busiest in Europe, after Heathrow.

We love that despite the global beat of the city's business districts, Frankfurt still feels like a small town. The city built green spaces before it was fashionable or deemed necessary. Frankfurt homes in the heart of town are endowed with front gardens, and city parks and woods can be found across the city.

Frankfurt city center after the Allied bombings of World War II.
Frankfurt 2006 FIFA World Cup celebration in the city center.

Well-being	9.5/10
Historical role	7/10
Attraction	6/10
Population	7.5/10
Dynamism	9/10
Average score	7.8/10

Patrick Bonneville: Amsterdam has many charms, among them, its permissiveness. But it is, above all, a chef d'œuvre of urbanism.

Amsterdam has been bustling since the late twelfth century, when it was a small fishing village along the banks of the Amstel River. It wasn't long before the small village grew to become an important port during the Dutch Golden Age of the 1600s. This period of prosperity and advancement lasted about 100 years, during which the Dutch were respected the world over for their skills in science, trade, and the arts.

Boats sailed from Amsterdam to all corners of the earth, fortifying Dutch leadership in sea trade. The States-General of the Netherlands began a new era in Western history when, in 1602, they granted the Dutch East India Company a 21-year monopoly of colonial activities in Asia. For all intents and purposes, this was the first multinational corporation. It was also the first company ever to issue stock. Its power was so great that it could virtually control government—it could wage war, negotiate treaties, coin money, and establish colonies. This led to the creation of the Amsterdam Stock Exchange, the oldest in the world.

Amsterdam eagerly embarked on the industrial revolution of the late nineteenth century, when important improvements in waterways and communications were undertaken. The Amsterdam-Rijn Kanaal was built as a direct connection to the Rhine, and the Noordzee Kanaal created a connection to the North Sea. These projects opened Amsterdam to new economic possibilities.

There is hardly a soul in the Western world who has not heard of Anne Frank. Born on June 12, 1929, Annelies Marie Frank became famous for the diary she kept while in hiding in an Amsterdam house during the German occupation of the Netherlands. The diary was found after she died and was subsequently published. The Anne Frank House is now a museum which was visited by over one million people in 2007 alone.

This was a time of a new social order, when riches were no longer reserved for nobility. Ordinary citizens could buy their way into upper-class society. In this sense, seventeenth century Amsterdam predates the American Dream. Thanks to the city's prosperity and role as a trade center, immigration was at a peak in the seventeenth century. Always the companion to overpopulation and its pests, the bubonic plague surfaced in Amsterdam in 1663. Although incoming ships were quarantined for at least thirty days, nothing could stop the spread of the disease, and an estimated 10 percent of the population died. Later in the century, city planners accommodated the growing population by building four half-circles of canals, ending at the IJ bay. This development resulted in the city we know today, which is a mere two meters above sea level.

Right: Replica of the *Amsterdam*, a 18th-century cargo ship with the Dutch East India Company.

When Amsterdam was liberated from Nazi occupation in September 1944, the city revived and flourished. Later, the city sailed through the cultural revolutions of the 1960s and '70s with great tolerance. While most other cities around the world frowned on the new youth culture, Amsterdam became the *magisch centrum,* or magical center, of Europe. It was a mecca of sorts for the hippie generation, who could easily and legally buy their soft drugs at legitimate businesses.

Today, an estimated 4.2 million people visit Amsterdam every year, making it the fifth most popular tourist destination in Europe. The city's population is 1.36 million; with its suburbs, it is over 6.5 million. A great many of these city dwellers use bicycles as their main transportation.

"In Amsterdam the water is the mistress and the land the vassal. Throughout the city there are as many canals and drawbridges as bracelets on a Gypsy's bronzed arms."
—*Felix Marti-Ibanez*

Well-being	8/10
Historical role	9/10
Attraction	9/10
Population	6/10
Dynamism	7/10
Average score	7.8/10

For tourists, Amsterdam offers open-air markets and rich architecture, including the Old Church, in the heart of Wallen, dating back to 1306. And the Beurs van Berlage, or stock exchange, is considered Holland's most important nineteenth-century architectural monument. Amsterdam Centraal and the Royal Palace are other notable sites. The city's canals and precise urban planning mean more than 100 kilometers of canals flow their way through the town, creating about 90 islands and 1,500 bridges. Amsterdam merits its nickname "Venice of the North."

We love the role Amsterdam has played in the evolution of modern economics and trade. We love that it is a haven for football fans and artists. And we love that Amsterdam has given the world Heineken and its notorious Red Light District.

"I'm proud to have been a Yankee. But I have found more happiness and contentment since I came back home to San Francisco than any man has a right to deserve. This is the friendliest city in the world."
—Joe DiMaggio, at his fiftieth birthday party

Patrick Bonneville: Subject to fires, fractured by tectonic shifting, and often blanketed in fog, this grand harbor city is set in an awesome natural environment. It is the city where gays have found refuge and where the United Nations Declaration was signed. Once you have lived in San Francisco, you cannot imagine living anywhere else.

Once upon a time, San Francisco was called Yerba Buena and was a Mexican territory. In 1776 the Spanish founded their Mission San Francisco de Asís, known as Mission Dolores, at this spot. It remained a port of Spain until that country granted independence to Mexico in 1821, heralding the end of mission services and the beginning of land privatization. The first settlement by an Englishman was at the homestead of William Richardson, in 1835. During the Mexican-American War, Captain John B. Montgomery claimed Yerba Buena and one year later, in 1847, the United States claimed the town and renamed it San Francisco.

Life in this coastal city during the late 1800s was prosperous and exciting. Nobody could have predicted the devastating event that awaited the citizens of this emerging metropolis on April 18, 1906. At 5:12 a.m., residents were awakened by a major earthquake. It was massive, registering 7.8 on the Richter scale, and caused damaging fires and aftershocks. More than 75 percent of the city was left in ruins, there were an estimated three thousand deaths and thousands more were left homeless.

Right: Aerial view of San Francisco in May 1906, just weeks after the fatal April 18th earthquake. More than 3,000 people lost their lives that day. The quake was caused by a rupture on the San Andreas Fault.

Politicians vigorously downplayed the damage from the 1906 earthquake for fear of widespread financial failure. In the following months and years, San Francisco was rebuilt to such tremendous economic stability that not a single bank failed in the 1929 stock market collapse. In fact, the city buzzed with activity during the Great Depression, when the Oakland Bay Bridge and the Golden Gate Bridge were built.

San Francisco was on the world stage as World War II ended with the signing of the charter that created the United Nations. This important document was drafted and signed in San Francisco in 1945; later, in 1951, the Treaty of San Francisco officially ended the war with Japan.

In the 1960s, "San Fran" was the hottest spot in the United States for music, good times, and political consciousness. In the Summer of Love, in 1967, hippies began to flood the city's Haight-Ashbury district to share poetry, fashion, and a spirit of freedom. A gay rights movement quickly evolved and with it came the election of Harvey Milk to the Board of Supervisors of The Castro—an urban gay village. Milk was assassinated on November 27, 1978, along with Mayor George Moscone. Both have become important symbols of the gay rights movement in the city, and indeed in all of America.

Along with several more earthquakes—big and small—the city eventually succumbed to financial failure in the guise of the dot-com crash. The late 1990s had seen an increase in computer-based companies in the San Francisco region, where cutting-edge developers and entrepreneurs had flocked with big ideas, big wallets, and big promises from their Internet companies. In the 2001 crash, companies folded, employees fled, and San Francisco was forced to reinvent itself. Only the strongest enterprises remained, and today the region is once again prosperous thanks to the technology industry.

Visitors and residents alike love the city for its hilly cityscape and mild, wet winters. San Franciscans love Baker Beach, now restored to a natural salt march ecosystem, and Ocean Beach, which skirts the Pacific Ocean. There, they can watch the surfers who brave its dangerous rip current waters. The city is loved for its cable cars and its permanent and manually operated cable car system—the last in the world. And it is loved for its "Painted Ladies," the Victorian and Edwardian buildings and houses embellished with multiple colors.

The most recognizable landmark of the city, of course, is the Golden Gate Bridge. Not only was it unique in its time for design and engineering, its chief engineer, Joseph Strauss, insisted on having a giant net installed beneath the bridge during construction—this saved the lives of nineteen workers.

We love that San Francisco was the home of American counterculture and the Summer of Love in 1967, when a hundred thousand people gathered at Haight-Ashbury in a spirit of hope and change. And we really love that Alcatraz is no longer a prison, but a national park that is open to visitors!

Well-being	9.5/10
Historical role	6.5/10
Attraction	9/10
Population	7/10
Dynamism	7/10
Average score	7.8/10

Patrick Bonneville: The fall of the Berlin Wall opened up this gem of Central Europe. Now, anyone can nourish their dreams with a visit to Prague's castles, churches, bridges, and narrow streets full of history and passion. No other city in the world looks as good under a fresh blanket of snow.

Prague has been loved by many of history's notable figures: the Roman emperors Charles IV and Rudolf II, Judah Loew ben Bezalel, Amadeus Mozart, Alfons Mucha, Jaroslav Seifert, Albert Einstein, and more recently, Barack Obama.

It is difficult to find a visitor who has not fallen in love with the "city of a hundred spires." *Praha,* as it is known in Czech, is the capital of the Czech Republic and is the country's largest city, with a metropolitan population of 1.9 million.

The history of Prague takes us back some 2.6 million years, where there is evidence of rudimentary human life in the region. Jumping forward to 500 BC, the Celtic tribe Boii baptized the region Bohemia and its river, Vltava. Much later, in the tenth and eleventh centuries, Bohemia began to attract an international reputation as a trade and religious center.

Well-being	7/10
Historical role	9/10
Attraction	10/10
Population	6/10
Dynamism	7/10
Average score	7.8/10

The Czech Přemyslid dynasty ruled most of Bohemia from 900 until 1306 AD. The first recognized prince, Bořivoj Přemyslovec, brought Christianity to the land. His wife, Ludmila, became a patron saint of Bohemia following her death. Prince Bořivoj moved Bohemia's center of power to Prague, and his castle became one of the largest inhabited fortresses in Europe. More than a millennium later, the same castle is still the seat of the Czech president.

Bořivoj's grandson became King Wenceslas, the honored king of the Christmas carol. He was dedicated to diplomacy and initiated communications with the Saxon dynasty; he felt Bohemia belonged in the larger Saxon empire as an equal partner. King Wenceslas is now the most beloved patron saint of the country, and his death is remembered with a national holiday every fall.

By the thirteenth century, the region around Prague Castle was granted town status. King Charles IV founded Charles University, the oldest Czech university as well as the first to be established in central, northern, and eastern Europe. Two hundred years of relative calm were enjoyed by the people as the monarchy was passed from father to son.

"Prague never lets you go... this dear little mother has sharp claws."
—*Franz Kafka, Jewish-Bohemian writer*

Right: Painting of Maria Church in Prague's Staromestska square.

Right: Sorrow at the Nazi annexation.
Far right: Famous historical Charles Bridge.

In 1576, Rudolf II ascended to the throne and brought a time of rebirth to the great city. Under his rule, Prague became the cultural center of the Holy Roman Empire, although shortly after his death the Thirty Years War fell upon the land and Protestants and Catholics battled for dominance.

Centuries passed and Prague was quiet. The seventeenth century brought about the golden age of Jewish Prague, as the Jewish population grew to comprise 30 percent of Prague's population. Queen Maria Theresa—who bore the titles of Archduchess of Austria, Queen of Hungary and Bohemia, Grand Duchess of Tuscany, and Holy Roman Empress— expulsed the Jews in 1745 because of their alleged collaboration with the Prussian army. They were only allowed to return three years later.

As Europe underwent democratic revolutions throughout the eighteenth century, a similar spirit aroused the Prague citizenry. Czechs opposed the German nationalist movement and began to show their colors. They gained majority in 1861, and in 1867, Emperor Francis Joseph I established the Dual Monarchy of the Austrian Empire and Kingdom of Hungary. The Austro-Hungarian Empire held sway until it was dissolved at the end of World War I and the sovereign state Czechoslovakia was declared in October, 1918. Prague, by then industrialized and with a population of 850,000, was chosen as the new capital.

World War II brought drastic change to all of Europe, and Prague was not spared. The Jewish community vanished, as almost every Jew fled for safety. The city slipped into communism and poverty. In the Prague Spring of 1968, political liberalization swept into the city amongst the wider spirit of liberalization and decolonization around the world. As Alexander Dubček's ideals took flight, however, he was stopped. In the terrible military mission called "Danube," numerous troops from the Soviet Union, Bulgaria, the German Democratic Republic, Hungary, and Poland invaded the Czechoslovak Socialist Republic. The invasion successfully stopped reforms and strengthened the authority of the Communist Party of Czechoslovakia. A dark period of industrial pollution, intimidation, and suppression descended upon the country and snuffed the light of Prague.

Twenty years later, after the fall of the Berlin Wall, peaceful demonstrators filled the streets of Prague in the Velvet Revolution. The Communists renounced power and Czechoslovakia was free. In 1993, once again, Prague became the capital of the newly defined Czech Republic.

There is much for both citizen and visitor in today's Prague. The Pivovar U Fleků is the world's oldest operating brewery; it dates back to 1499 and offers both delicious beer and rich history. The Prague Astronomical Clock, or Prague Orloj, is a medieval astronomical clock displaying elements of the sun, moon, planets, and the Apostles. The spectacular Charles Bridge, in its various constructions, has carried people across the Vlatava River since 1357.

It has connected the Old Town, Prague Castle, and the outlying regions since it was first built during the reign of King Charles IV. Its history is vital as a city built around immigrants and varied religions. Today's city dwellers are vital too. Prague's architecture and labyrinthine streets are lures into a world of classical music and charm, yet just across the street from the soul of ancient Bohemia is the contemporary urbanism of trendy shops, lively fashion, and vibrant nightlife.

We love the magical feel of Prague, with its Old World architecture and its opera-singing buskers on the Charles Bridge. We love the old Jewish Quarter, and we love the endless classical music concerts held for tourists in creaky-floored chambers and churches.

Patrick Bonneville: As the world entered the second millennium, a new city rose in the desert land. That city was Dubai. Suddenly, the region was of interest to everyone.

With over 1,4 million citizens, Dubai is the most populous state of the United Arab Emirates. According to census data, more than 1 million are male. This is likely due to a large immigrant workforce composed mostly of men.

Although Dubai is a relatively young city, human settlement of the land here is not. Evidence of life dates back to 3,000 BC. By the third century AD, the Sassanid Empire controlled the region, which was then passed into the hands of the Umayyad Caliphate in the seventh century. Islam was introduced during this period. The settlement remained a fishing and pearl diving community until it was established as a town in 1799. It remained relatively small and insignificant until 1966, when oil was discovered. The discovery of this black gold changed the course of Dubai forever.

Following the Persian Gulf War of 1990, Dubai made a giant leap forward in construction and development. Important projects not only brought a rise in immigration, they put Dubai at the forefront of creative construction.

Well-being	7.5/10
Historical role	3.5/10
Attraction	10/10
Population	7.5/10
Dynamism	10/10
Average score	7.7/10

The city is home to some very impressive structures, including the world's tallest freestanding hotel, the Burj Al Arab, and the Palm Islands, which are three artificial islands constructed in the shape of a date palm. The Palm Islands were built to host exclusive homes for the rich and famous, as well as a number of boutiques and businesses. Another impressive project is the World Islands, a huge man-made archipelago of three hundred islands that form a topographical image of the world.

Dubai today is a city of construction cranes. They represent jobs, expansion and wealth. The city has had some growing pains, however, as was evident during the economic depression of 2008. This low period hit the region hard and a number of projects were postponed or cancelled and many jobs cut. Human Rights Watch has issued a 71-page report that documents cases of serious abuse of construction workers in Dubai and in all of the United Arab Emirates. Abuse can take the form of extremely low wages, years of indebtedness to recruitment agencies (fees that UAE law stipulates must be paid by the employer, but are often not), withholding passports, hazardous working conditions, and brutally long work days.

Nevertheless, Dubai deserves recognition for having risen from the sands of the Arabian Desert to become a lush, prosperous region. The city attracts attention from the world's most influential bankers, investors, entrepreneurs, businesses, and entertainers.

We simply love the imagination that blossoms in this city. If it can be thought and bought, it can be built in Dubai.

"My grandfather rode a camel, my father rode a camel, I drive a Mercedes, my son drives a Land Rover, his son will drive a Land Rover, but his son will ride a camel."
—Sheikh Rashid bin Saeed Al Maktoum, founder of modern Dubai, worrying about the post-oil era

Left: Dubai under construction and (currently) the world's tallest skyscraper, the Burj Khalifa.
Above: The Burj Al Arab. It claims to be the most luxurious hotel in the world.

NORTH KOREA

Wonsan

Seoul

Chonju

SO
KO

Well-being	7/10	
Historical role	6.5/10	
Attraction	7/10	
Population	10/10	
Dynamism	8/10	
Average score	7.7/10	

Taegu

Patrick Bonneville: Seoul is dynamic, vibrant, growing, yet fragile because of its unpredictable neighbor, North Korea. The city is an example of achievement and success.

Seoul, Korea, is one of the world's largest cities, with a population of over 10 million. Factoring in surrounding areas, this number jumps to 24.5 million, making it the world's second largest metropolitan region. *Seo'ul* means "capital city" in the modern Korean language.

Left: Seoul, "Capital City" stands just south of the most heavily militarized border in the world, separating the two Koreas.
Above: Celebrating Chinese New Year in Seoul.

The Baekje Dynasty was a defining period for Korean culture, but it was during the Joseon Dynasty, in 1394, that the city was declared the capital of the country. It has remained so ever since. Six hundred years later, the city is picture perfect as mountains, rivers, and green spaces form a beautiful whole. Seoul is a city of traditional and modern cultures that blend so seamlessly that no effort to enjoy both is needed. City dwellers love the nearby mountains and, traditionally, believe them to be a path toward heaven.

We love Seoul for its rise to democracy and its vow to remain democratic. We love that relics of the city's past are lovingly cared for as statements of hope for its future. We love that the city is now one of the cleanest in Asia and is taking serious strides toward lowering air pollution. We love that the city has buses fueled by natural gas and an efficient and affordable subway system.

We love Seoul's 2007 designation as World Design Capital 2010 by the International Societies of Industrial Design—the city has one of the world's most technologically advanced infrastructures. It was rated number one on the *Digital Opportunity Index,* with the highest broadband Internet penetration of any city worldwide.

We love the city for its continued support of sports, art, and culture. It is home to more than one hundred museums, and Seoul also houses the World Taekwondo Federation headquarters. The Dongdaemun Market has been operating for over one hundred years, and the Namdaemun Market is the largest retail market in Seoul.

And, finally, we love the Hangang River. Seoulites begin their day along its banks with their morning exercise routines or gather there with friends. The city is proud of the river and its green spaces and the municipal government is continually "greening" other parts of the city, too.

Patrick Bonneville: This city and its citizens are leading the green movement, without looking back. No worries, there is no other city that even comes close. Some say Stockholm is filled with the best looking people in the world.

Above: Winter panoramic view of Stockholm.
Right: Typical street in *Gamla stan* ("The Old City")

Stockholm is the capital of Sweden and its largest city. It is the official residence of the Swedish monarch, as well as the country's Prime Minister. There are 818,603 people in the city, and about two million in the whole metropolitan region.

Founded around 1252, the settlements were built on a series of islets, or small islands. Legend and written texts speak of ruling families from as early as the first century, although the most reliable sources date the monarchy's history to the eighth century.

King Oscar I was a very liberal leader and during his reign, from 1844 to 1859, he introduced freedom of the press and equality of the sexes in inheritance law. These remarkable developments were a precedent: elsewhere in the West, in the mid-1800s, slavery was popular, politicians controlled the press, and women had few rights.

Stockholm played an important role in Sweden's raw-material and refined goods export trade. During the industrial revolution, the city was transformed and modernized, with electricity and even telephone connections equipping its buildings by the 1880s.

Today, this Nordic city ranks exceedingly high on quality-of-life indexes. There are some 450 sports facilities, including fourteen public indoor pools, and parks that make up about 30 percent of the city's area. There are at least 219 nature reserves surrounding the city, and a ten-minute metro ride is all it takes to get to the closest.

The European Commission named Stockholm the first European Green Capital 2010; by 2011, only clean vehicles will be allowed in the inner city, and Stockholm will be CO_2 free by 2030. Most of the jobs in Stockholm are in the service industry, which accounts for part of its greeness.

We love the fourteen islands the city is built upon, and their many bridges. We love the old town, *Gamla stan,* or "the city between the bridges." And of course we love Stockholm for its beautiful women, of whom there are some 20,000 more than there are men!

"The City will never be finished, it wil never be completed. It is constantly changing, being renewed and update At the same time, it is eternal; the pa somehow still remains, is preserved."
—Per Anders Fogelström, Swedish wri

Well-being	9.5/10
Historical role	8/10
Attraction	7.5/10
Population	6/10
Dynamism	7.5/10
Average score	7.7/10

Patrick Bonneville: I spent six months at York University, Toronto, in 1995. I was twenty years old. I met so many people there from all around the world. It was my first genuine contact with the world. Toronto is the Canadian financial center and the manufacturing hub for many big multinational companies. Its true identity, though, lies in its cosmopolitan genes. Toronto is living proof that the whole world can get along.

Toronto is the biggest city in Canada and the capital of the province of Ontario. The city has a population of 2.5 million, making it the fifth most populous city in North America. Including the metropolitan region, the population jumps to over 5.5 million.

Toronto reflects Canada's reputation as a tossed salad—there is a little bit of everything in this city. Current statistics show that 49 percent of Toronto's residents were not born in Canada. According to both the Economist Intelligence Unit and the Mercer Quality of Living Survey, Toronto is considered one of the world's most livable cities.

In the seventeenth century, Samuel de Champlain spoke of *Taronto,* or "the Narrows," a channel of water that ran through Lake Ontario into Lake Couchiching. The Iroquois called it *Tkaronto,* which means "where there are trees standing in the water."

Ontario incorporated the City of Toronto in 1834. By then, it was Upper Canada's largest town, with 9,250 people. The city had ambitious infrastructure projects, such as gas lighting, piped water, distinct neighborhoods for residential and commercial needs, as well as important public spaces such as St. Lawrence Hall and St James' Cathedral. This brought thousands of people to the town in search of jobs and a better life.

Canada gained independence from England in 1876 and Toronto set out to become a modern city. It developed

Above: Toronto streetcar running downtown near the CN Tower. The city has 11 streetcar lines.

industries and commercial, financial, and institutional networks in order to compete with Montreal's supremacy at the time.

We love Toronto for being the heart of Central Canada. This cosmopolitan city counts over 140 languages and dialects spoken on its streets and 200 distinct ethnicities living in its boundaries. Toronto welcomes about 25 percent of all new immigrants to Canada.

We love the young and dynamic spirit that resonates on its streets. It is the city with the most skyscrapers in North America, after New York City—Toronto has some 2,000 buildings over 90 meters high (300 feet) and New York City has over 5,000. We love the Royal Ontario Museum, which opened in 1912, and the Toronto Symphony, which was created in 1922.

We love the Hockey Wall of Fame that is located in Toronto. We also love the CN Tower, which stands at 553.33 meters. Downtown Toronto is also home to the Eaton Centre, a retail and office complex that sees about one million visitors every week.

Left: Celebration on Yonge Street in 1901.
Above: Toronto's financial center. Most Canadian banks are headquarted in Toronto. The Toronto Stock Exchange is the eighth biggest in the world.

And finally, we love internationally famous Torontonians such as Joe Shuster (the creator of Superman), John Candy, Mike Myers, Norman Jewison, Kiefer Sutherland, Morley Safer, Neil Young, the Barenaked Ladies, Deborah Cox, Alex Colville, Frank Gehry, Glenn Gould, David Cronenberg, and too many others to mention.

Well-being	9/10
Historical role	4/10
Attraction	7.5/10
Population	8.5/10
Dynamism	9/10
Average score	7.6/10

Patrick Bonneville: This grand city faced many challenges after the fall of the Soviet regime, but as the political and economic center of the largest country of the world, it has managed to overcome many of them.

Far left: Cathedral of Basil the Blessed, Red Square. **Left:** Moscow's International Business Center. **Below:** Red Square in 1802, by Russian painter Fedor Alekseev.

Moscow is the capital and largest city in Russia. Its population stands at roughly 10.5 million people, with nearly 15 million in its greater area. Classed as a megacity, it is the largest metropolitan area in Europe.

The city is named after the Moskva River, and residents are known as Muscovites, or *Moskvich* in Russian. The Kremlin, a World Heritage Site, serves as the residence of the President of Russia. As capital city, it is also home to the Russian parliament.

Moscow's written history begins in 1147 when it was founded by Russian Prince Yuri Dolgoruki. By 1328 the city was the capital of the Great Moscow Principality and the main city of all Russian lands. It held the title of capital until Peter I transferred the honor to St. Petersburg in 1713.

On March 12, 1918, Moscow became the capital of Soviet Russia and entered the annals of the twentieth century shrouded in the mysteries and secrets of Soviet Communism. Its citizens lived under this regime until the end of the Cold War in 1991.

Some important twentieth century dates for Moscow include the defeat of German forces in the Battle of Moscow in 1941, the Parade of Victory in the Great Patriotic War in Red Square in 1945 In 1965, the city was awarded the honorary title "Hero City" for its outstanding heroism during the Great Patriotic War. Moscow hosted the Olympic Games in 1980, and in 1991 the first freely elected mayor, G.Kh. Popov, was voted in. The fifth conference of the mayors of the major cities of the world was held in Moscow in 1997.

We love Moscow for its impressive collections of paintings, graphic art, and sculptures, including the Tretyakov Gallery and the museum of fine arts, named after A.S. Pushkin. There are 93 theaters, 94 cinemas, 23 concert halls, 61 museums, and 30 exhibition halls in Moscow. There are also 257 city universities, 60 state universities and academies, and an estimated 140 music and art schools for children alone!

We love Muscovites for their dedication to sports, a residual trait of the Soviet Union's sports system: there are 42 sports palaces, 92 stadiums, 8 cycle tracks, 245 swimming pools, 73 shooting ranges, 2,840 gymnasiums, 16 covered ice rinks with artificial ice, 39 ski lodges, 2,636 sporting grounds, 3 schools of higher sports mastership, 4 Olympic reserve colleges, 123 youth sports and Olympic reserve schools, and 5 sport education centers.

We love Moscow for its strength and inspiration as it has flourished with the new money of capitalism. In 2008, the city had 74 billionaires with an average wealth of $5.9 billion, although in 2009, this number dropped to 27; things are in flux in Moscow!

We love Moscow for its surprising, fantastic nightlife. We especially love Tverskaya Street, known as Gorky Street. And we love the city's subway system. It opened in 1935 and is a true museum in its own right, with spectacular art, mosaics, murals, and ornate chandeliers.

Well-being	6/10
Historical role	7.5/10
Attraction	7.5/10
Population	9.5/10
Dynamism	7.5/10
Average score	7.6/10

Patrick Bonneville: It would be a shame to write a book about the greatest cities in the world without underlining Nanjing's important journey. Invaded during World War II, then raped and massacred, the city was briefly broken. Now, the city is thriving again, playing an important role in China and in the world.

Above: Cityscape view of Nanjing.
Right: Wu Kingdom celebrations at the Gate of China in Nanjing.

As the capital of China's Jiangsu Province, Nanjing holds a very special place in Chinese history. It has been the capital of China twice during its lifetime and today serves as a reminder of royal history and an ancient culture. The city has a population of about 7.5 million people. Its name means "southern capital" (Beijing means "northern capital."). Nanjing could be the quintessential Chinese city: a perfect blend of monuments, politics, culture, and peace.

Nanjing was founded in 495 BC and was one of the original four great ancient Chinese capitals. The first emperor of the Ming Dynasty rebuilt the city and made it the Chinese capital in 1368; the city wall of Nanjing was built during his reign. Two hundred thousand workers took twenty-one years to build the wall, and when finished, it was the longest wall of its time.

Well-being	7/10
Historical role	10/10
Attraction	5/10
Population	9/10
Dynamism	7/10
Average score	7.6/10

The Nanjing Massacre, or the Rape of Nanking, refers to the Japanese attack and capture of the city in 1937. Thousands of civilians were murdered and tens of thousands of women were raped during the six-week period of Japanese control. An estimated 260,000 to 300,000 deaths were the result of the attack.

We love that today, Nanjing is ranked fourth by *Forbes* magazine in its 2008 "Top 100 Business Cities in Mainland China." The UN Habitat Scroll of Honor and National Civilized City award of 2008 went to the city of Nanjing. We also love its natural beauty. Flanked by mountains and nestled along the Yangtze River, the city features breathtaking scenery. It is also lucky enough to have natural lakes within its city center, such as the Xuanwu and Mochou Lakes. We love that Nanjing is a city of culture that attracts artists and intellectuals from all over China. The city also attracts great numbers of students who are looking for a world-class education in a traditional Chinese environment.

Patrick Bonneville: Madrid is the mother of the worldwide Hispanic community.

Madrid is the capital city of Spain. A recent census estimates the population to be 3.2 million people, and 5.84 million in the metropolitan area.

The oldest recorded mention of Madrid dates to the ninth century. Muhammad I of Cordoba had ordered a small palace to be constructed on what is today the Palacio Real. The city's name is believed to have evolved from the pre-Muslim word *matrice,* indicating the waters or stream in the area.

For many centuries, control of the region bounced between various rulers, including the Romans, barbarian tribes, and the Moors. In 1085, Alfonso VI conquered Madrid and ordered the mosque "purified" and consecrated as a Catholic Church under the guidance of La Virgen de la Almudena, who later became Madrid's female patron saint. During the fourteenth century, under the leadership of King Fernando V, the first Court of Madrid was assembled. This was also a period of expulsion of the "unbelievers"—the Moors and Jews.

The city grew rapidly during the eighteenth and nineteenth centuries, when castles, palaces, and cathedrals were erected to reflect the importance of the monarchy and the Church. Today, some of these buildings are still standing, although a devastating fire swept through the city in 1734 and destroyed many structures.

Above: La Plaza de Castilla and the Puerta de Europa towers, also known as the Torres KIO.

Below: Exterior of the city's largest railway station,the old Atocha Station. Early in the morning, on March 11, 2004, just a few meters from the crowded station, commuter trains exploded in a terrorist attack, killing 191 people and wounding 1,800.

"Not everyone is here; 191 are missing. We will never forget you."
—Two million citizens of Madrid and fellow Spaniards walked the streets of Madrid on March 12th, 2004, the day after the attack

The current king of Spain, Juan Carlos I, successfully oversaw the transition of Spain from a dictatorship under Franco to a parliamentary monarchy based in Madrid.

We love Madrid for The Puerta de Europa towers and for its parks, such as the Jardines del Buen Retiro, also known as El Retiro, the "Lungs of Madrid." We love Madrid's East Palace, and the downtown financial district. We love the Real Madrid Club de Fútbol and their fans. We love that Madrid holds strongly to tradition. Some are controversial—at the 25,000-seat Las Ventas bullring, fans can watch the world's best bullfighters toy with their prey. Madrid is considered the home of this Spanish tradition. Most of all, though, we love Madrid nightlife—with an afternoon siesta, it is quite possible to dine late, dance all night, go home to shower, and head straight to work the next morning!

Well-being	7/10
Historical role	8/10
Attraction	7/10
Population	8.5/10
Dynamism	7/10
Average score	7.5/10

Patrick Bonneville: Before this book, I didn't know Melbourne very well. I didn't expect it to be so big and so beautiful. Now I understand why when people speak of Melbourne, their eyes sparkle.

Melbourne is the capital of the state of Victoria and the second most populous city in Australia. Including the metropolitan region, the population in 2009 was about four million people. City dwellers are known as a Melburnians.

The original inhabitants of the area were the Wurundjeri people, of the Kunlin nation. They were badly decimated by disease, alcohol, and poor treatment by colonists. The city's European-era development dates to the mid 1800s with the construction of a bridge across the Yarra River. The Prince's Bridge, and then later the Queen's Bridge, were vital to the growth of the city.

Left: Looking at the city and Port Phillip Bay.
Right: Pathway in the Memorial Gardens, leading into the heart of the city.

The discovery of gold changed Melbourne. In the early 1850s, the precious ore was discovered in the state of Victoria and would-be prospectors used the city as home base to try their luck at the gold pits. Hopefuls arrived in droves, and the population boomed.

Melbourne was meticulously planned, even from its earliest days. Today, its early grid pattern remains. In 1878, when the city needed a market to accommodate the needs of its new settlers, the Queen Victoria Market was opened on the site of an old cemetery. It was a convenient location and so the bodies were relocated to the new Melbourne General Cemetery in Fawkner.

Australia's first steam-operated trains were established in Melbourne by the Melbourne and Hobson's Bay Railway Company in 1854. It was a single line that ran about four kilometers. In 1885, the first cable tramway opened, and by 1887, more than thirty-two kilometers of tramway were operational. The city was ready for the new century.

The Central Business District was developed just in time for the city to host the 1956 Olympic Games. After the success of the games, Melbourne entered the 1960s with optimism and great plans: the West Gate Bridge was built, the National Gallery of Victoria and the Victorian Arts Centre were opened, and many skyscrapers filled out the skyline.

We love that Melbourne acknowledges its role as home of the Kulin people, whose ancestors lived in the region for about 40,000 years. We love Melbourne for its moody weather; a favorite saying for the regions is "four seasons in one day."

We love the Eureka Tower, the world's tallest residential tower when measured to its highest floor. The Q1 building on the Gold Coast is officially the tallest residential building due to the spire added to its height. We also love the Royal Exhibition Building. Listed as a UNESCO World Heritage Site, it was built to host the Melbourne International Exhibition in 1880. It was the first building in Australia to receive a UNESCO designation.

We love that the first full-length feature film in the world was shot and shown in Melbourne in 1906. "The Story of the Kelly Gang" narrates the life of legendary Australian bushranger, Ned Kelly (1855-1880). It cost $2,250 to make and was banned from screenings due to its glorification of outlaws. Although only seventeen minutes have survived, the film was inscribed on the UNESCO Memory of the World Register in 2007.

Well-being	10/10
Historical role	5/10
Attraction	7/10
Population	8.5/10
Dynamism	7/10
Average score	7.5/10

"No city of the New Continent, not excepting those of the United States, presents scientific establishments so great and solid as those of the capital of Mexico."
—*Humboldt, 1803*

Well-being	6/10
Historical role	8/10
Attraction	6.5/10
Population	10/10
Dynamism	6.5/10
Average score	7.4/10

Patrick Bonneville: The big city of battles—or is it city of big battles? The Mexico City of the Aztecs was incredibly advanced for its day, and the Mexico City of the new millennium is no different.

This majestic city is one of the largest and richest in the world, with nearly nine million inhabitants. Figures for the population of the greater Mexico City area stand at around 19 million. *Ciudad de México*—Mexico City—was conceived in 1325, when it was built by the Aztecs on an island in Lake Texcoco. It quickly grew to be the largest city in all of the Americas. The Spanish conquered the city in 1521 and adopted it as the administrative center for the Spanish Conquest.

Flooding was a problem in old Mexico City; to remedy the situation, the Spanish drained the lake and built upon it. With its position between land masses to the north and south, and oceans on each coast, Mexico City was able to exploit the nation's riches and trade them in distant lands for luxuries such as silk or porcelain.

Mexico City was a turbulent place in the nineteenth century. After Mexico's fiercely won independence from Spain, in 1821, the city was captured by U.S. forces during the Mexican-American War, from 1846 to 1848. Later, there came more violence during the Reform War and the French Intervention, which led to the Mexican Revolution.

Left: Boulevard Paseo de la Reforma and the Torre Mayor skyscraper, the tallest in Latin America.

Today Mexico City is the third most populous in the world, with 19 million people. In 1968, Mexico City welcomed the world during the Olympic Games, which initiated a construction boom of over twenty new buildings and a subway system. As rural Mexicans migrated from their country villages to find a better way of life, the city's rapid population growth became difficult to manage. Water, waste management, and safety issues plagued the municipality. In fact, Mexico City began to sink, as the underground aquifer was depleted to serve its enormous population.

Mexico City suffers from a devastating pollution problem. Because of its extreme altitude, carbon monoxide and hydrocarbon released into the atmosphere are doubled and citizens suffer poor air quality for an estimated 334 days a year. Nevertheless, we love Mexico City for its fierce protection of its historical city center, including the Zócalo, one of the largest public squares in the world. We love Chapultepec, one of the biggest urban parks in the world. We also love the Xochimilco, the extended series of irrigation canals which are the vestiges of an ancient lake bearing the same name.

We love that it is one of the most liberal cities in Latin America. We love that it is home to a subway system that transports an estimated 4.4 million people every day. We love La Ciudad Universitaria; as one of the world's largest universities, it welcomes more than 270,000 students each semester. UNESCO declared the university a World Heritage site in 2007!

*Patrick Bonneville: Every single study in the world about quality of life comes to the same conclusion: Vancouver is **the** place to live. The city is relatively safe, beautifully squeezed in between the ocean and the Rocky Mountains, with an infrastructure and an economy to meet everyone's needs. The city is also strongly oriented toward the environment. For peace of mind and quality of life, the Canadian West Coast is the place to settle.*

Well-being	10/10
Historical role	4/10
Attraction	8.5/10
Population	6/10
Dynamism	8.5/10
Average score	7.4/10

Vancouver is the largest city on Canada's west coast, and the third largest in the country. It has a population of 578,041 people in the city proper and about 2,116,581 in the metropolitan region. The Economist Intelligent Survey of London describes the city as almost perfect, with petty crime and lack of affordable homes as Vancouver's only challenges.

Originally, this land was home to a group of First Nations people and was known as "S'ólh Téméxw." There is evidence of human life here dating back to 10,000 years ago. Spanish Captain José María Narváez landed in the region in 1791, followed by British naval Captain George Vancouver in 1792. Neither explorer settled, however. The area remained pristine until the late 1880s, when the Canadian Pacific Railway was completed and connected central Canada to the West. With the large numbers of Chinese workers hired to build the CPR, the city began to develop in force.

The first industry of any importance was the lumber industry. In 1863, a sawmill began operation at Moodyville, and from this grew a planned settlement and eventually a town named North Vancouver. An entrepreneur named John (Jack) Deighton arrived in 1867. A river pilot by trade, Jack decided a saloon was needed to quench the thirsts of the sawmill gang, and he set up shop on Alexander Street. Jack had the gift of the gab and soon garnered the nickname "Gassy Jack." Today, Gassy Jack's neck of the woods is known as Gastown.

The port of Vancouver was key to the development of the region. As the end of the line for the cross-Canada railway, it was literally a passage to Asia and Australia. Trade and shipping flourished. With the arrival of the Great Depression, Vancouver was badly hit by hard times. With thousands out of work and thousands more descending on the town in hope of finding work, crime exploded. As people joked at the time, Vancouver was the only city in Canada where you would starve to death before you would freeze to death. As with so many other cities worldwide, relief came with World War II. Suddenly work was abundant as industry flourished, and Vancouver shone for the next several decades. In 1986, Vancouver hosted the most recent World's Fair to be held in North America, Expo 86, which welcomed some 22 million visitors. The city enters the world stage once again, as host of the 2010 Winter Olympic Games.

We love Vancouver for its West Coast vibe of freedom. Vancouver has the greatest beach on the Canadian Pacific coast, a place where everybody fits in, regardless of who you are or where you're from. We love Stanley Park, all 404.9 hectares of it! It is 10 percent larger than Central Park in New York City and remains forested with over half a million trees that are hundreds of years old and that grow to an incredible 76 meters high (about 250 feet).

"It's a spirit about public space. I think Vancouverites are very, very proud that we built a city that really has a tremendous amount of space on the waterfront for people to recreate and to enjoy."
—Canadian architect and urban designer Bing Wing Thom

Left: Vancouver and the North Shore Mountains, reaching 1788m (5866 feet).
Above: Totem poles celebrating the the city and the region's Native heritage.

Patrick Bonneville: People come to Rio for the carnival, weather, beaches, nightlife, and for the thrill of feeling alive and active. It is huge, beautiful, and charming, but safety issues for citizens and visitors keep it lower on our list.

The megacity Rio de Janeiro, or simply Rio, has a population of 6,093,472 people, 14,387,000 including the metropolitan region. Its nickname is *Cidade maravilhosa,* the "marvelous city." Forbes Traveler recently rated Rio the happiest city on Earth.

Until 1960, Rio was the capital of Brazil. Before the country's independence from Portugal in 1825, Rio was the center of Portugal's New World colony. The city is situated among stunning mountains, vast beaches, and luscious rain forests—it is easy to see the attraction it held for Portuguese explorers landing in the area.

The Floresta da Tijuca, a hand-planted rainforest that covers about 32 square kilometers, is the second largest urban forest in the world. It is home to hundreds of species of plants and wildlife, many of which are threatened with extinction. The reserve was planted to replace natural rainforests that were eradicated for coffee plantations. It also serves as a means of protection for Rio's water supply. Rio's other great park, White Stone, is the largest native urban forest.

We love the city for its music and for its famous beaches, such as Copacaban and Ipanema. We love the zest that is palpable in the city and that is unparalleled. We love Rio's landmarks, including the giant statue of Christ, known as *Cristo redentor,* or "Christ the Redeemer." The statue was named one of the new seven wonders of the world.

"You walk off the plane in Rio, and your blood temperature goes up. The feel of the wind on your face, the water on your skin, the taste of the food, the music, the sexuality; Brazilians are very comfortable in their sexuality."
—American Actress Amy Irving

We absolutely love that Rio will host the 2016 Summer Olympics, the first South American city to host the event. We love that Rio is a sports town with a passion for soccer. The Maracanã stadium can hold nearly 199,000 people, as it did during the 1950 World Cup final. Due to modern safety regulations, though, officials no longer allow that many people in the stadium at once. There are five traditional Brazilian football clubs in Rio: the América Football Club, Botafogo, Fluminense, Vasco da Gama, and Flamengo. According to FIFA, Flamengo has the most supporters worldwide.

"In Brazil every kid starts playing street football very early. It's in our blood. As a professional I started at Sao Cristovao in the city of Rio de Janeiro. Of course I also played in the beach soccer league, barefoot."
—Brazilian soccer player Ronaldo

We love that Rio is home to the largest Portuguese community outside Lisbon and we love the presence of *pardos,* or "brown people"—a métissage of Whites, Blacks, and Amerindians. We love Rio's Carnival. The first festival was in 1723, though the modern version started in the 1930s. It is considered one of the biggest and greatest carnivals in the world. Participants prepare for the parade throughout the entire year, as the costumes are elaborate and large. We love that every year the festival is even more colorful and extravagant.

Left: Rio de Janeiro soccer championship. Second turn final game, Flamengo vs Botafogo, at Maracana Stadium, June 19 2009.
Above: The old Estádio do Maracanã, first opened in 1950 and renovated in 2007. It can welcome 103,000 spectators.
Right: A day at the beach in Rio.

Well-being	6/10
Historical role	5/10
Attraction	8.5/10
Population	9/10
Dynamism	8.5/10
Average score	7.4/10

Well-being	7.5/10
Historical role	8/10
Attraction	7/10
Population	7/10
Dynamism	7/10
Average score	7.3/10

Patrick Bonneville: The departure point for the discovery of the New World. It is the city of explorers.

Lisbon has about 2.8 million people, about 3.3 million including the suburban areas. It is the capital and largest city of Portugal. Lisbon is considered one of the world's oldest cities, with human settlements in the area dating to at least 300,000 years ago, and with evidence of residency by the Phoenecians and Greeks.

The Roman Empire controlled the city from about 205 BC, although when they conquered the town, it was already a thousand years old. Its placement near water and fertile land made the area popular, and Julius Caesar called it a *municipium,* under the name Felicitas Julia.

German tribes took control between the fifth and eighth centuries, then the Moors arrived in 714 and established roots that remained steadfast for over 400 years. Eventually the Moors were unable to resist Christian advances, and they lost out in 1147 to crusader Afonso Henriques, who conquered the city in the name of Christ.

Lisbon was an important European hub for commerce with Africa, India, the Far East, and later with the New World. Portugal also became an important commercial center for the slave trade and the textile industries. During this time of growth and construction, the Manuline style dominated architecture

and design. UNESCO has declared two such examples World Heritage Sites: The Belém Tower and the Jerónimos.

In the fifteenth century, Portuguese explorers traveled extensively around the known world, bringing back riches that would propel Lisbon, and Portugal, into the limelight. One such voyage would change history forever. Christopher Columbus's explorations of South America, North America, Africa, and Asia brought great prosperity to Portugal, and especially Lisbon. After Vasco da Gama mapped the sea route to India in 1497, Lisbon was crowned the world's most prosperous trading centre.

We love Lisbon for its important role in mapping the New World. We love that Lisbon was, and still is, a sea-proud city in a nation of sailors. We love Lisbon for rebuilding after a devastating earthquake destroyed most of the city in 1755. And we love the Portuguese culture that was born from a mix of peoples, food, and religion.

Left: The Padrão dos Descobrimentos Monument built in honor of the Portuguese explorers of the Age of Discovery.
Above: The red roofs of Old Lisbon.

Patrick Bonneville: An elegant and majestic European city. Many have fought for Milan. Everyone has wanted it at some point.

One mention of Milan, and images of the rich and famous and of fashion and design come to mind. It is the second largest city in Italy and the regional capital of Lombardy. The metropolitan area is estimated to have a population of 7.4 million Milanese, while the city center has about 1.3 million.

The Roman Empire conquered the region in 222 BC and named the village Mediolanum. The region was attacked, sacked, and conquered on more than one occasion before finally returning to Italy around 540 AD. Roman structures can still be seen in the city and some are still in use.

In the Middles Ages, Milan prospered as an important stop for traders journeying from Italy across the Alps. The city was again subjected to multiple claims of rule until 1861, when this and other regions were reunited and renamed the Kingdom of Italy.

The Germans occupied Milan during the Second World War. The city was a frequent meeting ground for battles between the Allied forces and the Germans, during which many beautiful structures were damaged. Some survived, however, such as the Gothic Milan Cathedral, the fourth largest in the world, and the Teatro alla Scala, inaugurated on August 3, 1778.

Below: Duomo di Milano. The construction of this magnificent cathedral began in 1386.
Right: Triumphal arch at the Piazza del Duomo.

The world famous La Scala was damaged by bombing but was rebuilt and still hosts opera's finest performers.

Metropolitan Milan has the fourth highest GDP in Europe; its economy is almost as large as that of Austria, a country that once ruled it! The city is the headquarters of fashion gurus from around the world – Gucci, Prada, Armani, Versace, and Dolce & Gabbana. The city is also famous for higher education; there are thirty-nine university centers that produce about 34,000 graduates each year, the largest number in all of Italy.

We love Milan for its architecture and respect for new and classic design. We love Milan for its nightlife and food and drink. We love Milan for its fashion industry, design sense, and its motor scooters.

Well-being	8/10
Historical role	7/10
Attraction	7/10
Population	7.5/10
Dynamism	7/10
Average score	7.3/10

"My cousin Francis and I are in perfect accord - he wants Milan, and so do I."
—*Charles V*

A VITTORIO EMANUELE II. I MILAN

Patrick Bonneville: The city of tango is the great lady of the South.

Buenos Aires is the capital and largest city of Argentina and the second largest metropolitan area in South America, after São Paulo. The name Buenos Aires translates to "fair winds." Residents of the city are called Porteños, or "people of the port." One in three Argentinians lives in the Buenos Aires region, and the population of the city and surrounding districts, in 2001, was recorded at just over twelve million.

Buenos Aires rose to its current stature largely due to its role in trade. For over two hundred years, traders on their way to Europe were obliged to pass through Peru so that Spain could collect taxes. Consequently, traders in Buenos Aires rebelled and began a successful contraband industry; Porteños also developed a resentment toward the Spanish authorities.

Former Argentinian President Juan Perón and his second wife, Spiritual Leader of the Nation of Argentina, Eva Perón, offered a glimmer of hope for citizens in this time. Peronism stood for a combination of nationalism and social democracy and a strong centralized government with authoritarian tendencies. After Perón's death in 1974, his wife became president. The right-wing paramilitary group Triple A, whom Eva Perón supported, had been in conflict with the left-wing revolutionary movement. This conflict led to the military coup of 1976, which then escalated to the "Dirty War." It was a dark moment in Argentinian history, when at least 30,000 people were kidnapped and killed by the military.

Today, the organization Mothers of the Plaza de Mayo works at keeping alive the memory of the *desaparecido,* or "those who disappeared." They have created an independent university, bookstore, library, and cultural center, and special projects offer free education, healthcare, and other services to the public. Their headquarters in Buenos Aires attracts important visitors each year.

Argentina gained its independence from Spain in 1816, but only after two unsuccessful British invasions. Then, in 1838 to 1840, French naval forces tried to take the city and failed. They teamed up with the British five years later for a second attempt and failed yet again. Both countries seem to have understood the resolution of Argentinians and left the country alone thereafter.

Above: Obelisco de Buenos Aires, located in the center of the Plaza de la República, the heart of the city.

Above: Tango sign on the renowned Caminito Street in the colorful neighborhood La Boca.

Buenos Aires was a popular destination for immigrants in the 1920s. As Spanish and Italian immigrants flooded Argentina, *villas miserias,* or shanty towns, began to spring up around Buenos Aires' industrial neighborhoods. This brought about serious social problems that were in stark contrast to the city's upper class image at a time when Argentina was considered one of the ten wealthiest countries in the world. As a result, by the time the Great Depression resounded around the world, Buenos Aires and Argentina were primed for civil unrest.

We love Buenos Aires for its warm climate and warm culture. We love the tango and the Teatro Colón, one of the world's greatest opera houses.

We love the city for its port and its trade industry, and for being the second biggest urban center in South America.

We love Buenos Aires for the Peróns and their dedication to democracy. We love the city for its European-influenced flavor and for its promotion of the arts, including cinema. We love the parks and we love Buenos Aires for its love of football—Buenos Aires has the highest concentration of teams in the world, with no fewer than twenty-four professional football teams!

Well-being	7/10
Historical role	7/10
Attraction	7/10
Population	8.5/10
Dynamism	7/10
Average score	7.3/10

Patrick Bonneville: L.A.'s setting is perfect: the Pacific Ocean to the west and the mountains to the east. This city embodies the American Dream for so many, providing opportunities that can't be found anywhere else.

Los Angeles is the second-largest city in the United States. It has a population of 3.8 million people but with the metropolitan region, the population jumps to 13 million residents.

According to Forbes, L.A. is the eighth most economically powerful city in the world. The Hollywood film industry helps the city qualify as the entertainment capital of the world. Crime issues in L.A. are so severe, however, that it is also sometimes known as the gang capital of the nation.

The city's history is riddled with violence. Between 1850 and 1870 there were thirty-five lynchings. L.A.'s murder rate hovered between ten and twenty times the annual rate for New York City during the same period.

Today, violence is mostly related to racial tension or gangs, although some incidents escalate from demonstrations that are inspired by politics, economic issues or sports.

Despite the violence, there is a lot to love about L.A. Hollywood is home to the most successful film studios in the world. The famous white-lettered Hollywood sign was created as an advertisement in 1923 and had such an impact that it was never taken down.

Left: Heavy traffic in Los Angeles. The metropolitain area has one of the world's strongest car cultures, with little public transportation. **Above:** Sunset on the Pacific Ocean in Santa Monica, in western Los Angeles County.

We love L.A. for its film and music industries and the dreams they make come true. We love the city for its native plants and wetlands. Urbanization and massive pollution seriously threaten these fragile ecosystems, so we would love L.A. more if it would put protection at the top of its priorities.

We love L.A. for its beaches, tourism, money, diverse cultures, near-perfect weather, museums, gardens, and parks.

"The location had all the requisites for a large settlement."
—Father Juan Crespí (1721–1782), after his expedition in the Los Angeles area

Well-being	7.5/10
Historical role	4/10
Attraction	8/10
Population	9.5/10
Dynamism	7.5/10
Average score	7.3/10

"A house full of people is a house full of different points of view."
—Maori proverb

Auckland is the largest and most populous urban area in New Zealand. It has 1.4 million people, which represents 31 percent of the country's entire population. It is the world's largest Polynesian city.

Dutch explorer Abel Tasman was the first European known to have seen the islands in this area in December 1642. Captain James Cook, so famous for his explorations in Australia, explored New Zealand in 1769. It was not long before Europeans were arriving in New Zealand by the hundreds, hoping for a new life in the timber and whaling industries. Europeans brought their way of life to the indigenous Maori, including muskets and disease. Many Maori lost their lives to these two devils of colonization, and the Maori unwittingly gave up their land, their resources, and their traditional way of life.

Auckland ranks fourth on the 2009 Mercer Quality of Life Survey. Summer weather has an average high of 23.7 °C, while winter weather is seldom cooler than 14.5 °C. With 2,060 hours of sunshine a year, it would appear as though every day is a perfect weather day. The city was cosmopolitan even before the word was trendy. Because it has always attracted people from all countries and all walks of life, by the late 1800s it was a city with dozens of languages and cultures.

Above: Marina in Auckland, "City of Sails."
Right: Karekare Beach Maori totem. The Maori were the first inhabitants of the region. The Maori population is over 600,000 in New Zealand.

The city is unique for its geographic location; it has harbors on two separate major bodies of water—the Tasman Sea and the Pacific Ocean. About fifty dormant or extinct volcanoes surround the city. Along with man-made structures, Auckland is a sports and outdoor enthusiast's dream come true: for trekking, bush walking, surfing, or just relaxing at the beach.

The city has a few challenges: the public transportation system is insufficient and leads to traffic congestion, and housing costs are on the rise, as is crime. These seem insignificant, however, when tallied against the high employment rate, mild climate, excellent education system, and an all round laid-back attitude.

Well-being	9.5/10
Historical role	7/10
Attraction	7.5/10
Population	5/10
Dynamism	7/10
Average score	7.2/10

"After the survey of the harbor. We next examined the land and timber around the Bay, and after three days careful investigation we located claims with a view of lumbering, and, ultimately, of laying off a town."
—Arthur A. Denny, pioneering West to build a new life and what would become the city of Seattle

Patrick Bonneville: If someone moves to Seattle for work or study, they might just never return. My closest cousin left Montreal with her husband for Seattle. I don't think they are coming back, and I can't blame them.

Seattle is known by many names: The Emerald City, Seatown, Rain City, Jet City, Gateway to Alaska, and Gateway to the Pacific. Only 154 kilometers south of the Canadian border, it is nestled between Puget Sound, on the Pacific Ocean, and Lake Washington. It was named after Chief Seattle, of the Duwamish and Suquamish tribes.

In 2009, there were 602,000 people living in the city and 3,345,000 in the metropolitan area. Seattle's history is tied to the ocean and to the indigenous people of the region. Due to its geographic location, it has always been a city with a bent for nature. Seattle also has a bent for education: it is ranked as one of the most literate cities in the Unites States, as well as the city with the most educated adults—an estimated 52.5 percent of residents hold at least a bachelor's degree.

"All things share the same breath - the beast, the tree, the man... the air shares its spirit with all the life it supports."
—Chief Seattle

Well-being	10/10
Historical role	3/10
Attraction	8/10
Population	7/10
Dynamism	8/10
Average score	7.2/10

We love Seattle for its pioneering spirit and for being stubborn enough to withstand at least five severe earthquakes in the span of a dozen years. We love that Jimi Hendrix was born in Seattle and that it is the city that gave the world grunge rock through its bands Nirvana, Alice in Chains, Pearl Jam, and Soundgarden. We love that the coffee company Starbucks started to build its worldwide empire of gourmet coffee shops in Seattle. We love Seattle for being the home of several other fantastically huge enterprises, including Microsoft, Boeing, and Costco.

We love Pike Place Market, the Space Needle, and the Fifth Avenue Theater. In fact, we love that Seattle has over two dozen live theater venues and about one hundred production companies. We love Seattle's love of the great outdoors. Its maritime climate means citizens spend time hiking, skiing, snowboarding, kayaking, rock climbing, sailing, swimming, walking, and boating. Downtown, they stroll around Green Lake or through Discovery Park, or beyond, along the shoreline of Lake Washington or into the Cascade and Olympic Mountains. Men's Fitness Magazine named Seattle the fittest city in the United States in 2005.

And finally, we love Seattle for its founder, Chief Seattle, to whom is attributed a speech in which he implored white settlers to respect his people and respect the environment around them. He was a wise man.

Right: Statue of Chief Seattle, called Si'ahl by his people, the Suquamish and Duwamish Native American tribes.

"Telegram received. I congratulate the citizens of Miami upon the harmony which marked the election yesterday and trust that the auspicious beginning will result in future prosperity which will equal the most sanguine expectation of the people of the new city."
—Henry Morrison Flagler (January 2, 1830 – May 20, 1913), founder of the Florida East Coast Railway and known as the father of Miami

Patrick Bonneville: The sun, the beach, the beautiful tanned people: those are enough to convert me to Miami. Add its Latino influence, flashy cars, and condo towers, and any visitor from a frigid climate is tempted to never leave the place. I call Miami "La Diablesse"— the Devil. The city is all passion and sensuality. It is temptation incarnate.

Miami has a population of 425,000 people. When we include the greater Miami area, the number jumps dramatically to 5.4 million residents. The United Nations places Miami as the fourth largest urbanized area in the United States, after New York City, Los Angeles, and Chicago.

The city dates back to 1896, but the Tequesta Indians lived in the region until the Spanish arrived in the sixteenth century. They were curious enough about the European newcomers to send their chief's son back with them to receive a formal education in Europe. As time advanced, the Tequesta disappeared.

Today, Miami is a cosmopolitan city that has a thriving tourism industry. People come to vacation and live in the area because of its sun, sand, and beaches. If Miami has a weak point, it is Mother Nature and her ability to turn a wonderful ocean into a hurricane nightmare. In 1926, Miami was destroyed by a hurricane that catapulted the city into a depression. It would take the Second World War to revive the city!

Miami's population grew after the war, and then again in the 1960s when a wave of Cuban refugees sought asylum in the city. About 125,000 refugees inundated Miami in four short months. In great entreprenurial spirit, many of them set up shops in order to serve those who were to come. Thus began Miami's current-day Latin connection.

Miami is determined to shed its crime-riddled image. A new program called the Quality of Life Task Force is the combined effort of several municipal departments to ameliorate the city and eradicate illegal activities. More than $500 million has been dedicated to vastly improving infrastructure, including the sewage and drainage projects in every Miami neighborhood. Yet another improvement project known as Midtown Miami will spend about $1.2 billion in commercial and residential development with the goal of creating jobs and economic stability.

ft: The Miami Beach Art Deco district is the largest **l**ection of Art Deco architecture in the world. **ove:** Miami skyline. Since the beginning of the **rd** millenium, Miami's skyscrapers have boomed: **r** 50 of them stand over 122 m tall (400 feet).

We love Miami's skyline, ranked the third most impressive in the United States, behind New York City and Chicago. In 2008, Miami was awarded the title "America's Cleanest City" by Forbes magazine. The city is proud of its good air quality, vast green spaces, clean drinking water, recycling programs, and excellent pollution control. We love the Everglades National Park to the west and Biscayne National Park to the east of Miami.

We love the Art Deco influence in Miami; there were over one thousand art deco buildings built between the 1920s and the 1940s. We love the Metromover, a free people-mover train serving downtown Miami and Brickell. And we love that about 66 percent of Miami residents list Spanish as their mother tongue.

Well-being	8/10
Historical role	3.5/10
Attraction	9/10
Population	8/10
Dynamism	7.5/10
Average score	7.2/10

Mumbai is the capital of the Indian state of Maharashtra and with its 14 million citizens is the second-most populous city in the world. The metropolitan region bumps this figure up to 19 million. Residents of the city are called Mumbaikars, Mumbaiites, or Bombayites. The sixteen major languages of India are represented in the city, and English is often the language of choice in the white-collar workforce.

Seven islands formed the area known as Bombay, which came to be controlled by several different empires during its long life. Under British rule, the city became an important central point for India's independence movement, which culminated with independence from the United Kingdom in 1947. Bombay was renamed Mumbai in 1996.

Mumbai is the major industrial and financial center of India. Because of the geographic location of the city, the population exerts great demands on existing infrastructures, and pollution and shantytowns are widespread. Until the 1970s, Mumbai relied heavily on the textile industry and its seaport for revenues, but commerce here has since diversified. Mumbai industries expanded to include high-tech companies, engineering, diamonds, and healthcare.

Current statistics show that there is an imbalance in the gender ratio in Mumbai: for every 1,000 males, there are only 774 females. Experts believe this is due to the large number of male migrants who come to Mumbai in search of work.

Above: Mumbai is often referred to as the "Island C

We love Mumbai for its role in India's fight for independence. We love Bollywood, the massively popular Hindi film industry. Headquartered in Mumbai, Bollywood is the largest film producer in the country. We love Mumbai for its favorite sport—cricket.

We love that the size, poverty, and pollution of Mumbai do not preclude beautiful inspiring moments and beautiful sights; they are a backdrop to a vast array of colors, sights, smells, tastes, and moments of connection with other humans. Mumbai is as international as cities get, and yet it remains purely Indian. We love that!

"It is at Bombay that the smell of all Asia boards the ship miles off shore, and holds the passenger's nose till he is clear of Asia again"
—English novelist and 1907 Nobel Prize winner, Rudyard Kipling

Well-being	4/10
Historical role	8/10
Attraction	7/10
Population	9.5/10
Dynamism	7/10
Average score	7.1/10

Left: Athens held the first and 28th Olympiads, in 1896 and 2004. The Panathenaic Stadium was used for both events. It is built of white marble.

A thens is the capital and largest city of Greece. It is one of the world's most ancient cities, with a recorded history at least 3,400 years old. The city itself has a relatively small population of about 745,514 people, but including the greater urban area, the population jumps to seventh place in the European Union with 4,013,368 inhabitants. Athens is the center of economic, financial, industrial, political and cultural life in Greece and is becoming an increasingly important city for the European Union.

It is virtually impossible to do justice to the history of this great town in a brief summary. It is one of humanity's first great cities, a place of democracy and philosophy, kings and goddesses, and rituals and morals. We love Athens and its 5,000 years of civilization. We love it as the birthplace of the Olympic Games. We love the city for its encouragement of fine art and literature. We love historic Athens and its ancient ruins, such as the Acropolis, the Ancient Agora, and the Roman Agora. We love that ancient Athens is integrated into the modern city, and how the urban development project called Unification of Archaeological Sites marries the old with the new.

But Athens is not just good for a journey back through time. We love contemporary Athens for its Gazi district—its trendy, artsy neighborhood—and the Kolonaki district, with its boutiques and high-end offerings. We love the weather and the blue sea at the city's feet.

We love the theaters of Athens. The city is home to 148 stages, more than any other city in the world. Shows can be seen at the ancient Odeon of Herodes Atticus, home to the Athens Festival and host to international singing stars.

Finally, we love that Athens does its best to improve the quality of life for its citizens. In 1991, the city began work on a subway system that would reduce the number of vehicles in the center of town and provide services to outlying regions that were in desperate need of attention.

"How great are the dangers I face to win a good name in Athens."
—Alexander The Great

Well-being	7/10
Historical role	10/10
Attraction	6/10
Population	7.5/10
Dynamism	5/10
Average score	7.1/10

Patrick Bonneville: If Boston is liberty's cradle and New York City its product, then Philadelphia is liberty's guardian.

Greater Philadelphia has a population of 5.8 million people, making it the United States' fifth-largest city. It has several nicknames including Philly, City of Brotherly Love, The City that Loves you Back, Quaker City, The Birthplace of America, and The City of Neighborhoods. These names should give you a good idea of why Philadelphia is on our list of the world's top cities.

Philadelphia played a vital role in the birth of the United States. It hosted the First Continental Congress, the Second Continental Congress—at which the fathers of the nation signed the United States Declaration of Independence— and the Constitutional Convention. Philadelphia was also the capital of the newly founded United States of America.

Although the city lost that title in 1800, it remained the nation's largest financial and cultural center for several years. It was the country's first major industrial city and was the largest manufacturer of textiles and home to major corporations. It was the hub for rail transportation, the host of the first official World's Fair in the United States and was the site of the very first brick house ever built in America, Penn House. Philadelphia was the first American city to officially plan a park for public pleasure, and was the site of the first school ever built in the United States. It was also the site of the first hospital in America, the Philadelphia Hospital.

We love Philadelphia for its role as the center of American history and American independence. We love Independence Hall. We love today's Philadelphia, including its manufacturing, healthcare, and other equally important industries. We love that Philadelphia has a strong and healthy economy, with its own Philadelphia Stock Exchange.

We love the typical red brick Philadelphia row houses. They began a construction trend across the entire country that was known as "Philadelphia rows." The homes are found throughout the entire city.

We love Philadelphia's political history. From the American Civil War through to today, the city has always held its banner proudly. For decades, its banner was that of the Republican Party, but in 1951 the city turned Democratic. In 2008, Democrat Barack Obama claimed a whopping 83 percent of the city's vote.

We love the city for its sports teams, such as the Phillies, the Eagles, the 76ers, and the Flyers. And we love the Philly cheesesteak sandwhich. The old, friendly rivalry still exists between Pat's Steaks, founded in 1930, and Geno's Steaks, founded in 1966. One thing is sure: no one else has cheesesteak like Philadelphia.

Right: The nickname City of Brotherly Love comes from Philadelphia's Greek roots, *philos* meaning "love", and *adelphos* meaning "brother." Philadelphia's LOVE sculpture was designed by Robert Indiana. Replicas of Philadelphia's landmark have been installed in at least 28 other cities all around the world.

Well-being	7.5/10
Historical role	7.5/10
Attraction	6.5/10
Population	7.5/10
Dynamism	6.5/10
Average score	7.1/10

Patrick Bonneville: Montreal is where I studied and began my career. My wife is Montréalaise. *My heart might be in New York, and my soul in the Green Mountains, but my history is in Montreal. I have great memories of this city. Montreal is the home of all Quebeckers; she is the mother ship of French-Canadian culture.*

Montreal is the second-largest predominantly French-speaking city in the world, after Paris. The population of greater Montreal was 3,635,571 in 2006. French is the mother tongue of 56.9 percent of the population, followed by English at 18.6 percent. The official language of the city is French, as defined by the city's charter.

Many believe Montreal's name dates back to Jacques Cartier's explorations of the area in 1535. He named the mountain that sits in the middle of the island Mont Réal, or Mont Royal in modern French. Geographer Battista Ramusio, who first mapped Montreal, spelled it in his native Italian as Monte Reale. The settlement that was established there in the 1600s was first called Ville-Marie, and for the original owners of the land, the Iroquois, the area was known as Hochelaga.

In 1802, Montreal was incorporated and granted the title of capital of the United Province of Canada. By 1860, it was the largest city in British North America and the economic and cultural center of Canada. By the turn of the twentieth century, it was a mostly francophone city.

Above: Raymond Mason's *The Illuminated Crowd* was created in 1985 and installed on McGill College Avenue, in the heart of downtown Montreal.

Prior to the British takeover in 1760, immigrants were required to be Roman Catholic; once under British rule, Montreal welcomed people of all faiths and the city grew to include many English companies. It wasn't long before the language of commerce was English.

The Scots were also active in early Montreal. They built the first bridge across the Saint Lawrence River, Morgan's department store—the first in Canada—the Bank of Montreal, Redpath Sugar, and both of Canada's national railroads. They also established McGill University and the Royal Victoria Hospital as well as a great number of industries.

Montreal has been the site of some politically charged uprisings, crises, and rebellions. These have often centered around the French-English debate. The language issue in Quebec is deeply embedded in the fabric of the land and in the emotions of its people.

We love Montreal for preserving its European heritage in its North American disguise. We love to hear French and we love to hear English and we love that Montrealers accept both. We love its citizens for protecting French in North America—without it, French in the New World would cease to exist.

We love the Montreal Canadiens and we love Montreal for being the mecca of ice hockey. We love the city's abundance of festivals and parties. We love Montreal's arts and music scene and Just for Laughs comedy festival. We love

the city's two French and two English universities. We love the Old Port with its romance, cobblestone streets, and artists painting on street corners, and we love the trendy Plateau district. We love Saint Joseph's Oratory's copper dome, second only to that of Saint Peter's Basilica in Rome!

We love that Montreal's pulse beats like no other city in Canada.

Well-being	8.5/10
Historical role	6.5/10
Attraction	6.5/10
Population	7/10
Dynamism	7/10
Average score	7.1/10

Below: Jacques Cartier Square in Montreal's Old Port in the early 1900s. This neighborhood remains one of the most vibrant places in the city.

Naples, or *Napoli* in Italian, is the capital of the Campania region and the province of Naples, in Italy. One of the oldest existing cities in the world, Naples is bathed in rich history and modern-day dynamism. The metropolitan region is home to about 4.5 million people and is the fourth most important city in Italy, in economic terms. Its historic city centre was declared a UNESCO World Heritage Site in 1995.

Naples was born some 2,800 years ago. Nestled between Mount Vesuvius and the Phlegraean Fields, it was first settled by the Ancient Greeks and then was later ruled by the Romans, Ostrogoths (a Germanic people), Byzantines, Spanish and again by the Romans.

Vestiges of its past can be found throughout the city. Ancient castles such as Castel Nuovo, Castel dell'Ovo and Sant'Elmo are attractions today, and a wealth of museums awaits the visitor to the city. The Naples National Archaeological Museum, widely considered as the most important Roman Empire museum in the world, houses many antiques from Pompeii and Herculaneum as well as a host of artefacts from the Greek and Renaissance periods.

Above: Because of the importance of the Catholic religion in its history, Naples is filled with over 100 beautiful churches, contributing to the city's spectacular architectural heritage.

Because Naples enjoys a Mediterranean climate and an ideal location in the bay of Naples, fresh food abounds. The city is famous for its beverages, both its award-winning wine industry and Neapolitan coffee. This is also the city that invented the espresso coffee machine. Eating is a favourite activity and the city is famous for its culinary traditions. The marvellous Italian dish of pizza originated in the city of Naples: originally a meal for the poor, under Ferdinand IV it became a traditional dish whose ingredients and cooking method were regulated by law. A real Neapolitan pizza was to be cooked in a wood-burning oven!

We love Naples for holding on to the stunning history of its gastronomy, architecture, and dialect. We love the city for its vibrant and unique culture. We love Naples for its contribution to music through the creation of the mandolin. We love that despite undergoing attacks during World War II, the city emerged and remained a beautiful model of Italian life. And finally, we love and thank Naples for pizza.

Well-being	7/10
Historical role	8.5/10
Attraction	6.5/10
Population	6/10
Dynamism	7/10
Average score	7.0/10

Above: Central Munich. The Frauenkirche, "Cathedral of Our Blessed Lady", is an important city landmark. Built in the 15th century, the cathedral can hold 20,000 people.

Patrick Bonneville: Sitting at the foot of the Alps and in the heart of Bavaria, Munich has played a key role in shaping Western, Central, and Eastern Europe.

On the River Isar, north of the Bavarian Alps, sits Germany's third largest city. About 5 million people live in Munich's metropolitan region. The city's official colors, black and gold, were the colors of the Holy Roman Empire; they have represented the city since the time of Ludwig the Bavarian, near the beginning of the fourteenth century.

Henry the Lion founded the city on June 14, 1158, and its status as a city was recorded for the first time in 1214. The city passed from religious rule to the rule of a duchy in the mid-1200s. In 1759, the Bavarian Academy of Sciences was founded in Munich and is still operational today. By 1806, the region had been in many wars and battles, but Munich was stabilized after Bavaria became the first German state with a written constitution in 1818.

The city had grown to about 500,000 inhabitants by 1901; film production flourished, the Hellabrunn Zoo opened in 1911, and the first television set ever exhibited in the world was put on display at the Deutche Museum in 1930.

In Nazi Germany, Munich was so infused with life and culture and the city had so much momentum that it was nicknamed Capital of the Movement [of the Third Reich]. Citizens were ready for the Americans when they arrived one April morning in 1945 to occupy the city, which lay in ruins due to Allied bombing. On that same day, in a bunker in Berlin, Adolf Hitler foresaw his end and committed suicide.

The city's motto is *München mag Dich,* "Munich loves you." And we love Munich! We love Oktoberfest, the sixteen-day festival that is one of Germany's most celebrated events and is the world's largest fair. It is not only an important exhibition of Bavarian culture, it is the biggest economic event for the entire region. We also love Munich for the Christmas market, which some sources say dates back to the fourteenth century.

Well-being	8/10
Historical role	8/10
Attraction	6.5/10
Population	7.5/10
Dynamism	5/10
Average score	7.0/10

"Today, in Ukraine, a new political year has begun. This is the beginning of a new epoch, the beginning of a new great democracy."
—*Ukranian President Viktor Yushchenko, December 2004*

Patrick Bonneville: Kiev showed to the modern world that it was possible to change regimes without violence. Thank you Kiev and the people of Ukraine for giving us hope in humanity. Thank you so much.

Kiev is the capital and the largest city of Ukraine. It has a population of nearly three million people. The city's documented history goes back to at least 600 AD. As a primarily Christian city since 988, it has prevailed through periods of extreme Orthodox Christianity, under Catholic Poland, and under the atheism of the Soviet Union.

Under Joseph Stalin's Soviet rule, Kiev suffered a horrific event known as Holodomor, or "death by starvation." In 1932 and '33, an estimated 2.5 to 10 million Ukrainians starved to death from the Soviet-led, politically motivated famine. There were no natural causes for it; in fact, the Ukraine had had a bumper wheat crop that year.

Kiev went on to win the title Hero City for its role during World War II, and it became an important center for the Soviet Union in the development and manufacturing of arms during the cold war. It came to specialize in aerospace, microelectronics, and precision optics industries. Upon the collapse of the Soviet Union in 1991, the Ukraine gained its independence and Kiev emerged as the capital city.

The Kiev of the new century is an important scientific and educational center as well as a major industrial pole in Eastern Europe. As industry makes its home here, Kiev is sure to move forward with improved infrastructure, public transportation, and employment.

We love today's Kiev for the old, such as the Saint Sophia Cathedral, and the new, such as the recently renovated Independence Square. We love Kiev's abundant green spaces and the brightly colored traditional dress of its residents.

Left: Yushenko kissing elected Prime Minister of Ukraine Yulia Tymoshenko at Central Square during the Orange Revolution in November 2004. The blood less revolution was a great victory for democracy. **Right:** Saint Sophia Cathedral dates from 1037.

Well-being	6/10
Historical role	9/10
Attraction	6.5/10
Population	7/10
Dynamism	6.5/10
Average score	7.0/10

Patrick Bonneville: It is an important accomplishment for humanity that Jakarta, the world's great Muslim metropolis, now democratically elects its leaders. August 2007 was an important step for Jakartans, and for all of us as well.

Jakarta is the capital and largest city of Indonesia. It has the biggest population of Southeast Asia, with some 8.5 million people in the city and about 24 million in the surrounding areas. Jakarta's nickname is the Big Durian, after the south-east Asian fruit, durian. The fruit's unusual odor and appearance are shocking to Western foreigners, as the city might well also be.

Jakarta's recorded history dates back to the fourth century when the area was a Hindu settlement. By the fourteenth century, it had become an important port for the Hindu Sunda Kingdom. The Portuguese came across Jakarta on their explorations for spice in 1511, and in 1522, the Portuguese signed a treaty with Pajajaran—the city's name at the time—in order to establish a trade port. Pajajaran served as an important trade city and was coveted by the Portuguese, Dutch, and Chinese. During World War II, Japan occupied Indonesia and named the city Jakarta.

The state gained its independence in 1950 and the city began a metamorphosis that continued into the new millennium. It has been a democratic, Muslim city since 2007. The city attracts much

Above: Jakarta's central business district and the Wisma 46, the tallest building in Indonesia.

foreign investment and many immigrants, which results in a city that mixes several languages, customs, and cultures into one important metropolis.

The city is marked by the contrast between the rich and the poor. Some neighborhoods have open sewers, not to mention violence and health issues. In these areas there is a dearth of police control as well. According to the World Health Organization, Jakarta is the third-most polluted city in the world, after Mexico City and Bangkok.

We love that Jakarta made its own choice for democracy.

Well-being	6/10
Historical role	8/10
Attraction	6.5/10
Population	8/10
Dynamism	6.5/10
Average score	7.0/10

Patrick Bonneville: Zürich might seem like a magical city in a fairytale setting. But beyond its looks, the city guards some of the world's most precious and secret treasures in its vaults.

Zürich is the largest city in Switzerland with a population of over 380,500 people, 1.9 million including the metropolitan region. Swiss German speakers make up the majority, with Italian-speakers making up nearly 5 percent of the population. It is known that the Romans had a military base in the region at about 15 BC and that they remained until about 400 AD. Other rulers included the Frankish Merovingians, Carolingians, and the Germans. Its freedom from occupation by outside powers was granted in the thirteenth century.

Zürich's modern facet is green—as in money. It is home to the world's fourth biggest stock exchange and it is Switzerland's financial capital. It is a city of banks, bankers, and foreign accounts. Switzerland's legendary banking regulations make it difficult for unauthorized people to gain access to information about account holders and their assets. This makes Swiss banking ideal for those who care about their privacy.

Above: Zürich in 1890. The city was built where the river Limmat pours into north-western Zürichsee, Lake Zurich, just 30 km (18 miles) north of the Alps.

The city is ripe with cafés, shops, restaurants, clubs, and fashion avenues. It is nestled along the River Limmat and the remarkably clean Lake Zürich. The city itself is visually stunning, with church steeples competing for the view with the hills, lake, and mountains. It is a crisply sensual feast for traditionalists and romantics alike.

We love that Mercer's quality of living surveys have consistently ranked Zürich as having the highest quality of life in the world, based on the city's economic growth. In 2009 it was second, after Vienna. Zürich has two universities and several colleges. The Swiss Federal Institute of Technology (ETH Zürich) and the University of Zürich are listed in the top fifty universities in the world.

We also love Zürich for its quality of life, atmosphere, safety, and its undeniable beauty.

Well-being	10/10
Historical role	7/10
Attraction	5/10
Population	6/10
Dynamism	7/10
Average score	7.0/10

Left: São Paulo is home of the Serra da Cantareira, the largest native urban forest in the world.

The city has always been an important center for culture and education. In 1935, the University of São Paulo was founded, and renowned foreign professors have taught there, including French anthropologist Claude Lévi-Strauss. São Paulo is the most ethnically diverse city in Brazil. There are over one hundred different ethnicities in the city.

São Paulo has the largest fleet of helicopters in the world and ranks third in the world for its number of skyscrapers, after New York and Hong Kong. We love that São Paulo is a major cultural center, with more than 12,000 restaurants serving about 62 different types of cuisine.

We are pretty sure that *paulistanos* do not love the city's potholes! The pothole situation in São Paulo is considered critical and poor maintenance means that the problem will not go away soon. Another very serious concern is crime, although according to the UN parameters of violence, São Paulo's crime rate has gone down over the last eight years.

Patrick Bonneville: I didn't know much about São Paulo. The first thing that hit me was the number of people who live there. I knew it was big, but I didn't expect it to be so huge!

São Paulo is the largest city in Brazil and the seventh largest metropolitan area in the world. It is the capital of the state of São Paulo, and the richest city in the country of Brazil. This megacity's population is over 11 million people, with a metropolitan population of 20,000,000. Residents are known as *paulistanos.*

Jesuit priests founded the town on the Roman Catholic day celebrating Saint Paul's conversion to Christianity. The priests chose the location in 1553 due to its "cold and tempered winds like in Spain" and "a healthy and fresh land and good waters."

Well-being	6/10
Historical role	7/10
Attraction	6/10
Population	10/10
Dynamism	6/10
Average score	7.0/10

Patrick Bonneville: True blue America and the kingdom of Coca-Cola.

Atlanta is the capital and most populous city in the state of Georgia. Along with Phoenix and Las Vegas, it is also one of the fastest-growing metropolitan regions in the United States. The city has a population of just over 530,000 people, which classifies it as the country's thirty-third biggest city. With the population of the greater area, however, the city jumps to eighth place, with over 5.25 million inhabitants.

The Cherokee Indians were the first inhabitants of this area, which they called Peach Tree Standing. Legend has it that the Europeans coming to the area began to use the word "peach" instead of "pitch," which referred to the sap that flowed from the large pine trees found in the region. Since peaches seemed to be a wild plant in the region, the peach stuck, and today Georgia is known as the Peach State. Today there are at least seventy-one streets in Atlanta with a variant of "peach tree" in their name.

The city itself was developed out of pure need; it was the end of the line for the Western & Atlantic railroad. Originally called Marthasville, in honor of the then-governor's daughter, the name was finally changed to Atlanta, after the railway that it served. The city is hometown to Coca-Cola, Home Depot, and Turner Broadcasting, Inc. The headquarters for AT&T Mobility is located in Atlanta, as are the headquarters for Delta Air Lines, Newell Rubbermaid, and UPS.

The city is home to the world's largest aquarium. The Georgia Aquarium was funded with a $250 million dollar grant from Home Depot co-founder Bernie Marcus.

We love that Atlanta is a city meant for living. We love the city of Atlanta for its role in bringing peace to America during the Civil War. We love that Southern traditions are not lost and forgotten here. And we love that Atlanta was chosen to host the 1996 Centennial Olympic Games.

Left: African-Americans make up more than half of Atlanta's population. The city played an important role in the 1960s civil rights movement. The mayor at the time, Ivan Allen Jr., supported the desegregation of Atlanta's public schools.

Well-being	8/10
Historical role	5/10
Attraction	6/10
Population	7.5/10
Dynamism	8/10
Average score	6.9/10

Patrick Bonneville: This grand city was built on the main route linking Asia and Europe. It is a bridge that has carried history, diplomacy, and bravery.

Istanbul, also known in history as Byzantium and Constantinople, is the largest city in Turkey. It is the fifth largest city proper in the world, with a population of 12.6 million people.

Above: People from diverse backgrounds and religions all get along in this multicultural city.

Byzantium was initially a Greek city named after King Byzas, or Byzantas, but its name was changed to Constantinople by the first millennium. Although Constantine the Great himself called the city Nova Roma, locally it was known by his name. Much later, on March 28, 1930, the city was officially christened Istanbul; Turkish officials requested that all nations use this name in their own languages as well.

Istanbul was the home of many kings, emperors, and sultans. Throughout its history, the city was the seat of power for many dynasties and empires, including the Byzantine, Roman, East Roman, Latin, and, finally, the Ottoman Empire. The city has been home to Christians, Muslims, and Jews who have for the most part lived in relative harmony.

When the Republic of Turkey was declared in 1923 by Mustafa Kemal Atatürk, Istanbul lost its title as capital city to Ankara. Nevertheless, in the following three decades, Istanbul undertook the refurbishment of many of its old, crumbling buildings. By the 1970s, the population began to grow as the city offered jobs and opportunities to newcomers. On August 17, 1999, an earthquake hit the region and left an incredible 18,000 dead and countless others homeless.

"If the Earth were a single state, Constantinople would be its capital
—Napoleon Bonaparte

ove: The Ortaköy Mosque overlooking the Bosphorus Bridge connecting Europe and Asia.

We simply love Istanbul for its former importance as Byzantium and Constantinople. We love Istanbul for its flora; the city has over 2,500 different natural plant species, more than in the whole of the United Kingdom. Some of these plants grow nowhere else on the planet!

We love Istanbul for its architectural heritage, including The Maiden's Tower, dating from 408 BC, the Hagia Sophia, the Palace of the Porphyrogenitus, and Topkapi Palace. We love the Grand Bazaar, one of the world's largest and oldest covered markets, which dates back to 1461.

We love the way Istanbul sits on the Bosphorus Strait; its incredible maritime infrastructure dates to the very foundations of the city, in the Roman era.

Well-being	6/10
Historical role	10/10
Attraction	7/10
Population	7.5/10
Dynamism	4/10
Average score	6.9/10

Patrick Bonneville: The diplomatic city of Europe and home of the European Union headquarters. A variety of cultures and ideologies meet here and show the world that differences do not matter when we share a common goal.

Brussels is the *de facto* capital city of the European Union (EU) and is the capital of Belgium, Flanders, and the French Community of Belgium. It is also the largest urban area in Belgium, with a population of 1.8 million people.

Since World War II, Brussels has become increasingly important in international politics. NATO and the EU both have their headquarters in the city and as a result, it has become a home for many other international organizations, politicians, diplomats, and civil servants.

The city is said to have been founded in 979 by Duke Charles of Lower Lotharingia. Brussels grew because of its location on the shores of the Senne, on an important trade route between Bruges, Ghent, and Cologne. By the eleventh century, marshes had to be drained to allow for more development. Two walls surrounded the city, and some of their remnants can still be seen in parts of Brussels.

A defining moment in the history of Brussels was the covering of the Senne. Since the river was extremely polluted and often flooded the lower residential neighborhoods, a plan to cover it was eventually accepted. In 1871, grand boulevards and modern buildings took its place.

Brussels has two official languages: Dutch and French. There are also about seventy thousand German-speaking residents. Tensions surrounding Dutch and French language laws abound, and although a separatist movement has the sympathy of many, opinion polls show that most Belgians want to keep their federation intact.

Brussels is home to 159 embassies and 2,500 diplomats. One-third of its citizens are foreigners and about 50 percent of the city's residents have a first language other than French or Dutch; consequently, the city has a remarkable cosmopolitan flavor. We love that Brussels welcomes immigrants and foreigners with open arms.

We love the medieval buildings that are mingled with modern constructions. We love the whispers of the past that echo over a leisurely cup of coffee in a public square. We love the Grand Place. And kids love the Mini-Europe Park; built to a scale of 1:25, it is filled with models of famous buildings from across Europe. We love Brussels for its waffles, chocolate, and even the Brussels sprout. And we love this city for becoming the home of so many important international organizations and efforts.

Well-being	7.5/10
Historical role	6/10
Attraction	7/10
Population	8/10
Dynamism	6/10
Average score	6.9/10

ow: Belgian flag floating in Brussels. The City of Brussels is the capital of Belgium. The Brussels Capi-Region, which includes the City of Brussels, is the *de facto* capital city of the European Union.

Patrick Bonneville: Central "DC" is a beautiful open-air museum that attests to power and responsibility. The city has seen great men and women rise up, supported by all Americans. The city has also seen others, who thought themselves great, fall. History is written in Washington every day.

Above: The Marine Corps War Memorial, also known as the Iwo Jima Memorial. In the background, the Washington Monument and the Capitol. The city is filled with monuments commemorating recent human and American history. **Right:** The American capital has witnessed key events that have influenced the course of history. On August 28, 1963, Martin Luther King, Jr. delivered his "I Have a Dream" speech, the high point of *The March on Washington for Jobs and Freedom.*

Washington, DC, formally the District of Columbia, is the capital of the United States. It was founded on July 16, 1790, and is a district of its own, not belonging to any state. The city is bordered by Virginia and Maryland. The resident population of the district is about 591,833 people, but with the addition of commuters, the population jumps to over one million during the workweek. The metropolitan area has a population of 5.3 million.

President Washington decided that the city would become the new location of the capital on November 21, 1800. He proposed naming the new capital Federal City, but a vote from commissioners led to the choice of Territory of Columbia, after Christopher Columbus; Federal City would be known as the City of Washington. Upon incorporation in 1871, District of Columbia officially replaced Territory of Columbia.

DC residents have fewer privileges of representation than residents of a state. They pay taxes, like all citizens of the country, but they do not have voting representation in the Senate or in the House of Representatives to protect their interests. It is Congress that reviews and stipulates DC regulations, and it is the President who appoints DC's judges.

"Washington is a city of Southern efficiency and Northern charm."
—*John F. Kennedy*

Every spring, citizens of Washington are greeted by a most beautiful sight along the Potomac waterfront: 3,020 cherry trees of twelve different varieties in full bloom. Following a series of visits to Japan, writer and photographer Eliza Ruhamah Scidmore had made it her mission to have cherry trees planted there. After more than twenty-five years of trying to generate interest in her project, in 1912 she had the trees shipped from Yokohama, a gift from the people of Japan.

We love Washington for its role as the political center of the United States, and its importance in American history. We love all the great speeches that have resounded from its impressive landmarks—the happy speeches, the inspiring speeches, and the ones that ended in tragedy. We love that Washington DC has embassies from almost every nation of this world.

Washington's safety record has not been a rosy one. It was once the murder capital of the United States. Since 2006, the crime rate has been dropping, and statistics show a decrease of about 50 percent.

We love Washington's role in the fight for civil rights and liberties. We love that this was the first American city with a majority African-American population.

We love Washington's parks. About 19 percent of DC is parkland. The parks hold some of the world's most famous monuments: the White House, Capitol Hill, the Washington Monument, the Lincoln Memorial, the Jefferson Memorial, and the Vietnam Veterans Memorial. There are about 71 museums in Washington DC, and many of them are free. Finally, we love the weather in Washington; it is almost perfect with four distinct seasons and balmy summers.

Well-being	8/10
Historical role	8/10
Attraction	6.5/10
Population	7/10
Dynamism	5/10
Average score	6.9/10

Patrick Bonneville: I remember when I visited Phoenix for the time in 2002. It was in July, and when the airport doors opened, my two-year old started shouting "Chaud! chaud! chaud!"—"Hot! hot! hot!"

Phoenix, Arizona, has several nicknames including Valley of the Sun and Bird City. It is a unique town at an elevation of 1,100 feet in the Sonoran Desert. The city has a population of about 1.5 million people, with just over four million in its greater metropolitan region. Even though the city is in the heart of a desert, it is well irrigated and is therefore a rich area for agriculture.

The Hohokam people lived in the region for at least one thousand years. Because rainfall is scarce and there is no snow, the only hope for life was in the Salt River. From it, Native Americans built an irrigation system of about 135 canals, making the land fertile for their agricultural needs. Eventually, however, Mother Nature prevailed, and after what is believed to be a prolonged drought, the area was abandoned.

The history of the city as we know it dates to about the 1860s, when Jack Swilling gazed upon the soil of the Salt River Valley. As had the Hohokam, he saw farmland that just needed water. He created a company that specialized in building canals and irrigation systems, and before long the land was green. By 1870, a town site was established that is, today, the downtown business section.

On July 4, 1887, while the United States was celebrating Independence Day, Phoenix welcomed the first Southern Pacific train to arrive in that city. Train service meant increased access to merchandise, greater trade opportunities, and the promise of added revenue. While Phoenix's economy was formerly based primarily on agriculture, cotton, and citrus farming, the city now also depends on tourism and high-tech industries. As the state capital, the government is also an important employer.

We love Phoenix for its dry climate—summer temperatures can reach 110°F (43°C). The record high on June 26, 1990, was 122°F (50°C)! City dwellers can escape the heat in its many parks, waterparks, and recreation centers. We also love that Phoenix is a haven for retired people; they flock to the city for the weather, the cost of living, the beautiful surroundings, and the golf courses. We love Phoenix for being a vibrant city in the middle of the American desert.

Well-being	9/10
Historical role	4/10
Attraction	7/10
Population	7/10
Dynamism	7/10
Average score	6.8/10

Left: Phoenix's old City Hall building. The city is so named because it is built on the ruins of a former civilization. It is the rebirth of humanity in the desert of Arizona.

Above: The Old Town Market of a city destroyed, left in ruins by the Nazi regime at the end of World War II.

Below: The Old Town Market rebuilt, now one of the city's main landmarks and tourist attractions.

"The city must completely disappear from the surface of the earth and serve only as a transport station for the Wehrmacht. No stone can remain standing. Every building must be razed to its foundation."
—*SS chief Heinrich Himmler*

Patrick Bonneville: Warsaw is a city like no other. The capital of Poland, the heart of a nation, it was completely destroyed, torn apart, with only dust and ruins left on the ground. Warsaw is a strong symbol of love and courage for all. This city is a portrait of what can come from the best and the worst of humanity. Everyone should know Warsaw's history.

Located on the Vistula River, Warsaw is the capital and largest city of Poland. It has a population of 1,700,000 people, about 2,785,000 including the metropolitan region.

Warsaw has seen war many times over. It was the site of battles in the sixteenth, seventeenth, and eighteenth centuries. But the 1700s also brought a period of great growth, in the guise of libraries, education, and economic stimulus, which bred hopes of independence from Russia. Finally, in 1918, Poland gained its independence.

On Adolf Hitler's march to domination, he didn't sidestep around Warsaw. Caught between the Soviets and the Nazis, the city was a clear target in Hitler's sights, and in September 1939, the city succumbed to German occupation. Warsaw's Jews received the brunt of Hitler's ire.

In the 1943 Jewish Ghetto Uprising, a whole district was annihilated and half a million people massacred. Not long after followed the 1944 Warsaw Uprising. The Nazis issued a death sentence for Warsaw—every person was to be sent to the concentration camps and every brick was to be destroyed. Everything was lost: libraries, museums, collections, churches, palaces, and homes. In all, some 650,000 people were killed and 84 percent of the city was destroyed.

The only thing Hitler did not expect was that he and the Nazis could not destroy Varsovians' spirit, and in 1945 the rebuilding of Warsaw began under a Soviet-led Communist government. Important historical and cultural structures were reconstructed to be as they were before the war. They are in the city's Old Town, now a UNESCO World Heritage Site. In 1989, Poland had its first democratic elections, marking the end of the Communist regime.

Well-being	6/10
Historical role	8.5/10
Attraction	5.5/10
Population	7/10
Dynamism	7/10
Average score	6.8/10

Above: Panorama of a proud modern city. Since the fall of the Soviet regime in 1989, Warsaw has become an emerging economic leader in Europe.

We love Warsaw for its perseverance in the face of violence and oppression, and for rebuilding itself from the smoldering ruins of World War II. We love Warsaw for its important role in many international agreements, including the Warsaw Pact, the Warsaw Convention, and the Treaty of Warsaw.

We love Warsaw for underpinning Polish culture in its ballets, operas, theaters, and restaurants. We also really love the symbol that has appeared on the city's coat of arms for at least 500 years: the Warsaw Mermaid.

"There was no difficulty in finding Warsaw. It was visible from 100 kilometers away. The city was in flames and with so many huge fires burning, it was almost impossible to pick up the target marker flares." —William Fairly, a South African pilot, from an interview in 1982

Patrick Bonneville: From the early days of Ancient Egypt, Cairo has had a strong impact on the rest of the world and the cities yet to come.

Left: Sailboat on the Nile River, the heart of the city.
Right: Preserving a rich history and heritage.

Cairo is the capital of Egypt and the largest city in the Middle East. The city itself is only about one thousand years old, but the region surrounding Cairo is much older. Humans have created some of the world's most famous monuments and structures in the lands surrounding Cairo that date back as far as written history reaches.

Modern Cairo is a megacity with a core population of 6.5 million people and another 10 million living in its surrounding regions. To overcome its sheer size, Cairo has developed important mass transportation systems. The fast and efficient metro system of this Muslim city includes some trains that have cars dedicated exclusively for women, should they choose to sit separately from men. Just recently, the city unveiled a new ring road that allows drivers to circle around the outskirts. Driving in Cairo is known to require both patience and aggression—traffic can be fast and furious!

We love the history of the famous river the city is situated upon, the Nile. So much culture and so many religious symbols were born of these waters. The city sits in the shadows of former glory, not far from the Nile Delta. Cairo was held by Romans, Muslims, Ottomans, the French, and the British. Finally, in 1922, Egypt gained its independence, and from there it began to grow in importance as a central point of the modern Arab world.

We love the romance that the history of this land imparts to Cairo. We love that this city is a place where Western and Middle Eastern ideologies meet. We love that there are at least sixteen higher education institutions in Cairo, including the second oldest university in the world—Al Azhar University opened its doors in 975 AD.

We love Old Cairo. Remnants of its history line the small streets and alleys, and ruins of churches and Roman fortifications are common. There are the Coptic Museum, the Babylon Fortress, and the Hanging Church to appreciate, as well as the Ben Ezra Synagogue and the Mosque of Amr ibn al-'As.

We love Cairo's nickname—*Um ad-Dunya*, or "mother of the world." And if you want to love Cairo, may we recommend just sitting, with a sweet *shai* in your hand, watching life buzz here as it has for centuries.

Well-being	4/10
Historical role	10/10
Attraction	7/10
Population	9/10
Dynamism	4/10
Average score	6.8/10

Taipei is the largest city in the Republic of China (not to be confused with the People's Republic of China), otherwise known as Taiwan. It has been the *de facto* capital since 1949. It has a population of over 2.5 million people in the city and about 10 million in the greater city area.

Long ago, Taipei was a lush, wet region where people would gather along the banks of the lake to fish or make pottery. It was a mountainous region, much like today, with a lake instead of a town center as a meeting place. The lake slowly drained away about three hundred years ago, and a city of streets was born.

The Spanish, Portuguese, and Dutch each had periods of control of the island; an historic Spanish fortress still stands in Danshui. In 1709, China moved in and forbade settlement to non-Chinese citizens. Japan took the city briefly, from 1895-1945, and in 1949, Taipei fell back under complete Chinese control. When Mao Zedong created his Peoples' Republic on mainland China, the Republic of China was relegated to Taipei and the island of Taiwan. The city grew quickly, and its infrastructure was soon insufficient for its population.

Today, Taipei is one of Asia's most livable cities. It has become a global player in the technology sector, producing many of the components needed for the industry. In 2009, Taiwan had over $321 billion in foreign exchange reserves, unemployment was virtually non-existent, and the city had a very low inflation rate.

We love that Taipei Metro delivers efficient services with both a subway and a light rail system. Users travel with EasyCards, which work like gift cards; each time a card holder travels, the amount of the fare is reduced from the card. Scanners at the entrances to buses and metros can even scan the card through a purse or wallet!

We love that there are twenty university campuses in Taipei, including National Chiao Tung University, Taiwan's oldest, established in 1896. We also love its attraction to western-style sports, especially baseball and basketball. We also love the modernism of Taipei, including its Taipei 101 Tower. The city has the fastest elevator in the world. It has been said that Taipei is old enough to feel its past, yet young enough to get WiFi all over town.

Well-being	6.5/10
Historical role	5.5/10
Attraction	6/10
Population	9/10
Dynamism	7/10
Average score	6.8/10

Left: Built in the Taipei Basin, the city is surrounded by hills and mountains.
Right: Taipei 101, formerly the world's tallest building.

Oslo is the both the capital and the largest city in Norway. It has a population of 1.4 million in the metropolitan region.

King Harald III of Norway founded the city in 1048. Since that time, it has grown to be the cultural, scientific, economic, and political center of the country. It relies heavily on maritime industry; an estimated 8,500 people are employed by some 980 companies related to maritime ventures.

Oslo is currently one of the most expensive cities in which to live. According to the Globalization and World Cities Study Group and Network, as of 2008 Oslo is a major world city and one of Europe's fastest growing metropolises, with a 2 percent rate of increase annually. About one quarter of the city's residents are immigrants.

We love the moderate climate from the mild influence of the Gulf Stream and the city's emphasis on green spaces and parks. Because of careful planning, all parts of the city are within a short distance of forests.

We love that Oslo's public transportation system includes a successful bicycle rental program that has been operating since 2002. The city is a transportation hub for the rest of Norway. Access into the city requires the payment of a toll, and the collected funds are used to finance new public transportation projects.

We love that the Norwegian Nobel Committee hands out the Nobel Peace Prize every year in Oslo. Several Norwegian authors have received the Nobel Prize for literature; this is a reflection of the important role literature plays in Norwegian culture.

Well-being	9/10
Historical role	6.5/10
Attraction	7.5/10
Population	3.5/10
Dynamism	7.5/10
Average score	6.8/10

Left: Norwegian troll holding the flag of Norway. Trolls are an integrated part of Scandinavian folklore and Norwegian literature.
Upper left: Oslo street and houses.
Above: The Vigeland Sculpture Park, featuring 212 sculptures, is the lifework and legacy of sculptor Gustav Vigeland.

"The Creator made Italy from designs by Michelangelo"
-Mark Twain

Patrick Bonneville: Florence is a mythical city. Florence gave inspiration to the great artists who enlightened our world.

Illustrations from past centuries show a town so strikingly similar to today's that it is as if time stopped in Florence. This city of history and romance is known as *Firenze* in modern Italian, and is the capital of Italy's Tuscany region.

The Golden Age of Florentine art began around 1000 AD, during a period of great luxury and wealth in the city. In the centuries that followed, churches, basilicas, castles, and galleries were adorned with the artwork that gave Florence its enduring magnificence.

When the Black Death floated over Europe like a fire's thick smoke, Florence was not spared. A booming town of 80,000 prior to its advent, in 1348, the plague cut the city's population in half.

It would take nearly 150 years for Europe to recuperate from the infectious disease, during which time the de'Medici family rose to greatness. Florence was forever influenced by the power of this family, and it is thanks to Lorenzo de' Medici that Florence became the center for Renaissance art—both then and today. "Lorenzo the Magnificent" commissioned works by all of the great artists of the time: Michelangelo, Leonardo da Vinci, and Botticelli.

The de' Medici family lost power in the early eighteenth century and when Austria gained the town in 1737, the region of Tuscany found itself under Austrian control. In 1861, Tuscany became a province of the United Kingdom of Italy and its capital in 1865. To modernize Florence, and to make it worthy of its new position, medieval buildings were torn down and replaced with a formal street plan and newer houses.

Above: The Arno River crosses Florence, passing below the Ponte Vecchio and the Santa Trìnita bridges.
Right: Florence is the art capital of Italy, and features some of humanity's most important works. It is the best preserved Renaissance center of art and architecture in the world.

German forces occupied Florence during World War II, and as they retreated, they began to destroy all bridges into the city. Remarkably, Hitler ordered German troops not to destroy the Ponte Vecchio—he deemed it too beautiful. Allied soldiers who died defending the region were buried in cemeteries just outside the city.

We love Florence for being the "cradle of the Renaissance" and for its conservation of its medieval heritage. We love that Florence is a symbol of delectable Tuscan food, developed from simple peasant traditions and from the inspirations of the garden.

"Aristotle was wrong; the universe was made out of five elements, not four: Earth, Air, Fire, Water, and Florentines."
—Pope Boniface, 1300

Well-being	8/10
Historical role	7/10
Attraction	9.5/10
Population	5/10
Dynamism	4/10
Average score	6.7/10

Patrick Bonneville: Hamburg is all about the sea. There is one common element characterizing the growth of the city: the port, the port, and the port.

Hamburg's official name is "The Free and Hanseatic City of Hamburg." It is Germany's second largest city with a population of 1.8 million people, 4.3 million including the metropolitan region. It receives about 7.4 million visitors each year.

Hamburg's history began in the most humble of ways, as a mission. Its purpose was to convert the Saxons to Catholicism. Hamburg grew to become an important trading center for Europe, and its port secured its position for centuries.

One interesting bit of Hamburg's trivia is the status of its swans. In 1264, the Hamburg Senate enacted a law to protect the swans of the Alster River. It was widely believed at the time that, as long as the swans were free and living on the Alster River, Hamburg would be free and remain prosperous in the Hanseatic trade alliance. Anyone who beat to death, insulted, shot, or ate a swan would receive a harsh punishment. The birds have been fed regularly since the sixteenth century, and by 1818, a special keeper was assigned to move the swans to a special ice-free location for the winter. Today, about 120 swans spend their summers on the Alster.

We love Hamburg for its size—not the population, but the land. With its 755 square kilometers, Hamburg city is 7 times larger than Paris and 2.5 times the size of London. This alone makes the quality of life in Hamburg particularly high.

We love the city for its stubbornness in maintaining its role as an important shipping port throughout its history, during wars, takeovers, plagues, and economic crises. We also love that Hamburg had the courage to rebuild after the devastating Allied attacks of World War II.

We love Hamburg's canals and more than 2,300 bridges—more than Amsterdam and Venice combined. We love its theaters, museums, music venues, and clubs. We love that there are over 8,500 companies engaged in cultural enterprises, such as the performing arts, literature, and music. The Beatles claimed Hamburg was their training ground; in 1960, they played a 48-day gig at the Indra Club and then packed their bags and moved down the street for another 58-day gig.

t: Hamburg in 1150, a few years before it joined the powerful Hanseatic League.

ɔve: The historic warehouse district of Hamburg.

Finally, we love Hamburg for its sports: Hamburg is sometimes called Germany's sports capital, as it is home to more first league teams and international sports events than any other German city.

"I reported for the first time orally to the Fuehrer that if these aerial attacks continued, a rapid end of the war might be the consequence."
—*German Minister of Armaments and War Production Albert Speer, commenting on the Hamburg attacks*

"I might have been born in Liverpool - but I grew up in Hamburg."
—*John Lennon*

Well-being	8.5/10
Historical role	6/10
Attraction	9.5/10
Population	5/10
Dynamism	4/10
Average score	6.7/10

Helsinki is the capital and largest city in Finland. The population is just over half a million people, with about 1.3 million including the metropolitan region.

Finland was under Swedish control for centuries, and so Helsinki, originally a trading post, was founded in 1550 by King Gustavus Vasa of Sweden. Due to its location, the city was an important military site during the many Russian, Baltic, and German wars.

Finland was not far from Russia's eighteenth century capital, St. Petersburg. As Russia was gaining both political and economical importance during this time, it was virtually inevitable that it was to occupy Helsinki. Indeed, the city fell under Russian rule during the Great Hate of 1713-21 and then again in 1742. Sweden's status as a superpower had dwindled and the loss of Helsinki was a great blow. In order to regain the city, Sweden built the seafortress Suomenlinna, and this move brought increased prosperity and trade to the region.

In 1818, after almost two centuries of war and occupation, Helsinki became the capital of Finland. Helsinki native Johan Albrect Ehrenström and German-born architect Carl Ludwig Engel are responsible for the Helsinki we know today, a city of Empire architecture and Neo-Renaissance style. By the early 1900s, the city had a population of about 100,000 and was an important political and industrial center for the region. After

World War I, Finland declared itself an independent nation, and in World War II, the Soviet Union attacked but never occupied the country. Finland was thus one of the few European countries to hold on to its independence during the war.

Helsinki deserves mention for its research institutions. It counts eight universities, six technology parks, and it is an important hub for research, business, and government. Helsinki also has a reputation as a center for ethics in research. The Declaration of Helsinki, originally adopted in 1964, is a guide to ethical practices for the medical community.

We love the architecture in Helsinki. Whether you prefer the prestigious plans of Ehrenström and Engel or the Art Nouveau influence of the early 1900s, the city is as romantic as it is functional and as beautiful as it is convenient.

We love the city for its love of sports. Helsinki hosted the Olympic Games in the summer of 1952.

Right: Aerial view of the compact city. Its 19th century urban design is the work of the architect Carl Ludvig Engel. The reconstruction of the city center was the grand final signature of the German architect.

Well-being	8/10
Historical role	6.5/10
Attraction	6.5/10
Population	4.5/10
Dynamism	7.5/10
Average score	6.6/10

Well-being	6.5/10
Historical role	7.5/10
Attraction	7.0/10
Population	6.5/10
Dynamism	5.5/10
Average score	6.6/10

Patrick Bonneville: My first contact with the East was one day spent in Budapest in 2001. I couldn't resist; one year later I was back to drink in the charm and inspiration of the city.

Budapest is the capital and largest city of Hungary. Greater Budapest has a population of 3,3 million. In 2008, it ranked third out of sixty-five on Mastercard's Emerging Markets Index and was named the most livable Central/Eastern European city on EIU's quality of life index. An incredible 20 million visitors are welcomed to the city every year.

Every era of Budapest's spectacular history is written in the souls that roam its streets. Historically, the area was at an important crossroads on the shores of the Danube, at a junction where travelers could soak in the hot springs before continuing on their trade route. Today's Budapest was created in 1873, upon the unification of three cities along both banks of the Danube River: Buda, Óbuda, and Pest.

ft: The Gothic Matthias Church, the heart of Hun-
ary, built in the center of Buda's Castle District.
bove: The spectacular Gothic Hungarian Parliament
uilt on the Danube shore in Pest.

Modern history saw Budapest as capital of the Communist People's Republic of Hungary. In the Hungarian Revolution of 1956, the city fought for democracy and freedom from its Communist regime. The revolution meant death for many freedom fighters—some estimates have up to 10,000 dead or missing—and an estimated 200,000 Hungarians fled the country. In 1956, Time Magazine listed "the Hungarian freedom fighter" its Man of the Year. In 1989, as the Soviet Union dissolved, Hungary rejected Communism.

We love the beauty of the Buda hills, the Danube, and the bridges that cross it. We love the public baths and the more than 130 natural thermal springs and wells in Budapest. We love the courage of all the men and women who fought for freedom and who paved the way for democracy for other Eastern European nations. We love that Budapest strives for a fair government, which is housed in one of the most beautiful parliament buildings in all of Europe.

We especially love that through their hardships, Hungarians have remained positive and optimistic. "Goulash Communism" is a perfect example of this resilience: named for the typical Hungarian dish of hodge-podge ingredients mixed into a meal, the idea represented the mixed ideology that ruled Hungary until 1989. Although they were officially communist at the time, they enjoyed many liberties that were prohibited in other Eastern Bloc nations.

Santiago is the capital and largest city of Chile, South America. The most recent census put the metropolitan population at just under 6.7 million people. This number represents a whopping 36 percent of the country's entire population.

Santiago is considered to be an alpha city, meaning that it plays an important role in the world's global economic system. It is home to major industries, cultural establishments, and educational institutions and serves as a vital transportation hub for the entire South American continent.

The city was founded on February 12, 1541, by the Spanish conquistador Pedro de Valdivia. War between the Inca and the *Conquistadores* had lasted several years and ended only when the Inca moved south, away from this region, in 1542. The city quickly grew due to abundant vegetation in the region, an ideal climate, and its ideal location at the Mapocho River.

The first railroad opened in 1857 and made the city easily accessible and open to trade with other regions of the country and the continent. By the 1930s, industry had begun to transform Santiago into a modern metropolis. In the 1970s, new legislation was put in place to reduce the effects of poverty in the city; measures were taken to increase workers' wages, control rent increases, and offer free health care and free shoes and milk for every child.

While we don't love the city's smog problem, we love Santiago for its thirty-three educational institutions, including the University of Chile, which first opened in 1622. We love the city's soccer teams and its two orchestras. We love that Santiago has adapted to the needs of its citizens, creating fair work conditions and expanding transportation routes to open itself to trade and industry. We love its geographic portrait and we are hopeful Santiago's citizens will strive for a healthier environment in the years to come. The prestigious mountain ranges and waterways that surround this city deserve protection from pollution.

Well-being	6/10
Historical role	6.5/10
Attraction	6/10
Population	8.5/10
Dynamism	6/10
Average score	6.6/10

Upper left: Modern downtown view at sunset.
Above: Santiago against the Chilean coastal range o a day of low smog.

Left: Jin Wan Square on the Hai River shore. The river played an important role in the devolpment of the city, connecting it to Beijing and to the Yellow Sea.

Tianjin is China's sixth largest city in terms of urban population, with over 11.5 million residents. The city does not belong to a provincial body; instead, it is an independent city that reports directly to the federal government. As such, Tianjin enjoys a lifestyle unlike most Chinese cities.

The city is located along the Hai He River, which connects to the Yellow and the Yangtze Rivers. Tianjin has been a city since 1725 and was opened to international trade after the end of the Second Opium War in 1858. This brought the construction of schools, hospitals, and other public institutions. Many of those original buildings are still standing today. The city seemed under constant attack as Britain, Japan, France, America, Austro-Hungary, and Italian forces all vied for control. In 1902 the city returned to Chinese power, and in 1927 it was officially established as a municipality of China. On July 30, 1937, Tianjin fell to Japan and, consequently, to American rule following the end of World War II. In 1949, Communist forces took the city and it was returned to China.

Today, farmland is an important source of revenue for Tianjin, taking up about 40 percent of the area's land for mostly wheat, rice and maize. Tianjin does not have the infrastructure capital that other major Chinese cities have, so it suffers from a lack of some services, including water. A further challenge for city dwellers is dust, which seems to be everywhere.

The city cleaned up prior to the 2008 Olympics, destroying run-down buildings, modernizing the public transportation system, and expanding roads into broad and breezy avenues. A new bridge spans the Hai River and modern office towers line the streets. There are still little homes whose courtyards, nevertheless, are filled with chickens, rabbits, and geese!

We love that the city is famous in China for its stand-up comedy scene and that the city has a lively and well-respected performance-art culture. This boosts the reputation of Tianjin's citizens as humorous, open, and uncomplicated.

Well-being	6/10
Historical role	6.5/10
Attraction	5/10
Population	9/10
Dynamism	6.5/10
Average score	6.6/10

Patrick Bonneville: Hangzhou is about beauty first, then heritage, and, finally, prosperity. It might not have the international fame of Beijing, Hong Kong, or Shanghai, but it ranks in our top-100 list because it plays a very important role in China and in the world as well.

Above: The sun-shaped Hangzhou Peace International Exhibition and Conference Center.

There are close to 4.0 million people living in the Hangzhou metropolitan region. The city is renowned for its spectacular natural surroundings, its West Lake, and the incredible Hangzhou Bay Bridge. Located at the southern end of China's Grand Canal, which extends north to Beijing, the city was visited by Marco Polo, who reported it to be "beyond dispute, the finest and noblest in the world."

Hangzhou was founded during the Qin Dynasty, about 2,200 years ago. The city of the Sui Dynasty (591 AD) era is now considered one of the seven ancient capitals of China. Today, the city's economy is thriving. Ideally situated near Shanghai, the city is abuzz with various industries, including agriculture, textiles, and tourism. It is a large manufacturing base that serves as a hub for coastal China.

Hangzhou is said to be the incarnation of Xi Shi, one of The Four Great Beauties of ancient Chinese lore renowned for their charm. According to legend, their beauty held such great influence over kings and emperors that they caused the decline of kingdoms.

We love the West Lake, a freshwater lake located in the historic center of the city. It has been the center of Hangzhou life for centuries and is the subject of many poems, paintings, events, and stories. We also love the Xixi National Wetland Park, the first and only national park of its kind in China. The wetlands' 1,800-year history is woven into Chinese culture.

Last but not least, we adore the Hangzhou Bay Bridge. Opened to the public on May 1, 2008, after a whole year of intensive safety testing, it is the longest trans-oceanic bridge in the world. It measures 35.673 kilometers (22 miles). The bridge is shaped like an "S" so that the annual Silver Dragon tidal bore will not be diminished by its presence.

Well-being	5/10
Historical role	7/10
Attraction	6/10
Population	7/10
Dynamism	7.5/10
Average score	6.5/10

Houston is the largest city in the state of Texas and the fourth largest in the United States. The 2008 U.S. census recorded a population in the metropolitan region of over 5.7 million people.

This city was incorporated in 1837, a year after its founding by the brothers Augustus Chapman Allen and John Kirby Allen, real-estate entrepreneurs. At the time, the area was known as the Republic of Texas and was under the direction of General Sam Houston. The city became an important region in the country after the discovery of oil there in 1901.

Houston was built near the Buffalo Bayou waterway, which led to the creation of its successful maritime industry; this, in turn, led to the success of the rail industry here. Houston has also drawn important air and space organizations, such as NASA's shuttle programs, because its agreeable weather provides near ideal conditions. Unfortunately, the city is prone to hurricanes and tropical storms. In 2001, Tropical Storm Allison was responsible for the worst flooding in the city's history, and in 2005, nearly 2.5 million people were evacuated as a precaution for oncoming Hurricane Rita.

Well-being	8/10
Historical role	3.5/10
Attraction	5.5/10
Population	7.5/10
Dynamism	7.5/10
Average score	6.4/10

Right: Downtown skyline. Most of the city's skyscrapers were built in the 1970s and 1980s.

The city of Houston leads the housing market in the United States, with an impressive 42,697 building permits issued in 2008. The city is widely considered the energy capital of the world, with five of the six super-major energy companies basing their American operations here. But Houston is also a city of museums and the arts. An example of its dedication to culture is the annual Houston International Festival which highlights a different culture each year.

We love Houston for being a multicultural city: over ninety languages are spoken on its streets. We love the city for its exciting history. We love that Houston diversified during the oil crisis of the 1970s to embrace other industries such as medical and scientific research and development. We love that NASA chose Houston as mission control. We love the Texas Medical Center, the world's largest. It has forty-seven medicine-related institutions that include thirteen hospitals, two specialty institutions, two medical schools, four nursing schools, and schools of dentistry, public health, pharmacy, and other health-related practices. All of its institutions are non-profit. Most of all, we love that the citizens of this vibrant city welcomed thousands of New Orleans refugees in the wake of Hurricane Katrina.

Patrick Bonneville: Such a proud city, Edinburgh is full of history and wisdom. If Glasgow is the heart of Scotland, Edinburg is the soul and the spirit of Scots worldwide.

Edinburgh lies on the east coast of Scotland along the Firth of Forth, near the North Sea. It is easy to see why so many people feel it is one of the most picturesque cities in Europe. Its medieval and Georgian architecture sit alongside some of the most impressive cliffs and rugged landscapes of Great Britain.

The city has only 472,000 people, 773,000 including the surrounding areas, but it welcomes over a million tourists every year; Edinburgh's population triples itself in tourism. The city's nickname is Auld Reekie, Scottish for Old Smoky—a reference to the days of coal and wood heating when chimneys spewed thick smoke into the air. As with the history of England, Edinburgh's history is tied intrinsically to the country's past. Rebellion, plagues, murder, miscarriages of justice, monarchs, and invasions all color the city's heritage.

The name Edinburgh is derived from the fortress Din Eidyn, or "Edwin's fort" in the Brythonic language. Edwin was King of Northumbria from 616 to 632. The collection of homes around the castle evolved into the name Edwinesburch, and eventually, into Edinburgh.

In the fifteenth century, King James IV of Scotland moved the Royal Court to Holyrood, in Edinburgh. In 1603, King James VI took the throne of England and Ireland, and established the Parliament of Scotland in the Great Hall of Edinburgh Castle. Parliament moved again to Tolbooth, then to Parliament House, which now houses the Supreme Courts of Scotland.

Above: Traffic on Princes Street.
Right: The Edinburgh Castle at sunset.

Well-being	7/10
Historical role	9/10
Attraction	6.5/10
Population	3.5/10
Dynamism	6/10
Average score	6.4/10

King James VI united England and Scotland under one monarchy—although not politically—upon the death of Queen Elizabeth I in 1603. He then became King James I of England. Politically, the two countries merged one hundred years later under Queen Anne, in 1707. Scotland remained a separate country within Great Britain, with Edinburgh as its capital.

Edinburgh was walled for defense purposes, and as a result of the confined space, houses and workspaces had to be built upwards. While elsewhere in the seventeenth century it was uncommon to see multistory buildings, in Edinburgh there were several buildings at least eleven stories high. In the nineteenth century, Glasgow, to the west, embraced the industrial revolution and grew to become an important industrial, commercial, and trade center. Edinburgh remained the intellectual and cultural center of the country.

Edinburgh is still one of the United Kingdom's cultural capitals. The world renowned Edinburgh Festival, held over four weeks every summer, unites several smaller official and independent festivals. These include the Edinburgh Military Tattoo, the Edinburgh International Book Festival, and the Edinburgh Fringe, the largest performing arts festival in the world. About half a million tourists and visitors make the effort each year to attend the festivities.

We love Edinburgh for its proud and rich history. We love the Old Town and the New Town. We love that Edinburgh fought for its independence from England and remains united on its values and culture. We love the people of Edinburgh and their conviviality, easily shared with friends and strangers alike. Most of all, we love that Edinburgh was voted the most desirable city to live in the UK by a 2009 YouGov poll.

Above: The Moorish Islamic architecture of Plaza de España.
Lower right: Matador during the *corrida*, bullfighting, a popular traditional event in Seville.

This city in southern Spain is the financial, artistic, and cultural capital of Andalusia and the province of Seville. The name conjures images of dancing and music, food and drink, and beautiful women in bright dresses who bring music to life.

Seville is situated on the plain of the River Guadalquivir, with an average elevation of seven meters (twenty-three feet) above sea level. Residents are called Sevillanos (for men), Sevillanas (for women), or Hispalenses. In 2008, there were 700,000 people living in the city, and 1,450,000 in the metropolitan area.

Legend speaks of the city's founding by Hercules. The city is believed to be over 2,000 years old and was occupied by the Romans, Moors, and Muslims. During the exploration period of human history, Seville's riches grew tremendously as it profited from the discovery of the New World. It remained a prosperous city until the Great Plague swept through in 1649, and about 50 percent of Seville's citizens perished. The population did not recover until the early 1800s.

We love Seville for its Mediterranean climate and for its long and varied history. We love the city for its parks, among them, the Parque de María Luisa that was built for the 1929 World's Fair. We love the Gardens of the Alcázar that have graced the city for centuries. The site was once a Moorish fort; it is an amazing palace still used by the Royal Family and is now a UNESCO World Heritage Site.

We love the Seville Semana Santa. Sevillanos celebrate the end of Holy Week with a two-week party! We love La Feria de Sevilla, the city's April fair, and its parades and flamenco dances. We love Seville's nightlife and its food and its delightful atmosphere.

Well-being	7.5/10
Historical role	7/10
Attraction	5/10
Population	7.5/10
Dynamism	5/10
Average score	6.4/10

Patrick Bonneville: Visitors love the city at least as much as the locals. Nobody leaves Copenhagen with a bad impression.

Copenhagen is the largest city and capital of Denmark. It has a population of 1,167,569 people, with another 700,000 in the surrounding areas. The city is built on the islands of Zealand and Amager.

Copenhagen is a large city with a small-town atmosphere. Its history is rich in art, commerce, and trade. One thousand years ago, the city was nothing more than salt marshes and small inlets with a small trading center. Today, it is a center of commerce and research and development and was named by FDi magazine as one of the top five "future cities of Europe."

Well-being	8/10	
Historical role	7/10	
Attraction	5/10	
Population	7/10	
Dynamism	5/10	
Average score	6.4/10	

In the 1990s, Copenhagen set about restoring its historic districts to their once unequalled glory, and many restoration projects included environmentally friendly updates.

In fact, we love Copenhagen for its dedication to the environment as it ensures clean water, provides adequate bicycle paths, and an abundance of green spaces for its citizens. Denmark was the first country in the world to establish an environmental law, in 1973. Copenhagen received the European Environmental Management Award in 2006. We love the wind farm that was built off the coast of Copenhagen at Middelgrunden and that now produces about 4 percent of the city's energy.

We love the way the city has developed its suburban areas in a "five-finger" plan that allows for an efficient mass transportation system. Most of all, we love the little mermaid statue in the Copenhagen harbor, a statue of a mermaid sitting on a rock that has been a tourist attraction since its creation in 1909.

Upper left: Colorful 17th century Nyhavn Canal, a popular Copenhagen landmark.
Above: Middelgrunden, an offshore wind farm which provides more than 3% of the city's power.

Lyon is the second-largest metro-politan area in France, after Paris. There are 1,8 million Lyonnais, and with their suburban counterparts, the city's population jumps to over 4,4 million people.

Lyon was founded as a Roman military colony in 43 BC, when it was named Lugdunum. From this capital, Augustus ruled the Roman territories known as the Three Gauls. It remained a quiet town until the fifteenth century when the city became the most important print and publishing center of the time.

By the mid-eighteenth century, the city was booming. Silk weavers made up about 40 percent of the workforce; in 1830, when they had had enough of their poor work conditions, including eighty-hour workweeks and poor air, they began to strike. Several hundred workers were killed by the time the strikes ended. Lyon was also the site of horrific war crimes during World War II. Four thousand people were killed and another 7,500 were sent to Nazi death camps at the hands of Gestapo chief Klaus Barbie.

We love the city of Lyon for its contribution to the world of cinema. In 1870, the Lumière brothers shot the first moving picture. Their subjects were workers leaving their father's photographic factory.

Right: Lyon in the mid-19th century, an era when the city faced an historical workers' uprising and became a powerful industrial force in Europe.

We love that Lyon is notable for its food and drink: two of the most re-spected wines are grown in the region: Beaujolais to the north and Côtes du Rhône to the south. The city is known in Europe for its traditional dishes of Lyon sausage, *andouillette, coq au vin,* sugared chestnuts, pike quenelles, tripe cooked with onions, and *salade lyon-naise* (lettuce with bacon, croutons, and a poached egg).

We love that Lyon has been a serious player in the commercial, industrial, and banking world for the past five hundred years. It is a city of spectacular museums, lively culture, and a great nightlife. Lyon offers world-class edu-cation and sophisticated shopping. It is a city with parks, winding paths along the riverside, and an historic old town.

Well-being	8/10
Historical role	6/10
Attraction	5/10
Population	7/10
Dynamism	6/10
Average score	6.4/10

Chengdu is the capital of the Sichuan province in the southwest People's Republic of China. It is the most important economic center of the area. The metropolitan region has a population of around 11 million people, making it China's fifth largest city. In 2007, according to the Public Appraisal for Best Chinese Cities for Investment, Chengdu was chosen as one of the top ten cities out of two hundred and eighty urban centers in China.

The land surrounding the region, which is highly fertile, is called *Tianfuzhi guo,* "the country of heaven." The city has lived through the perils of dozens of dynasties since its founding in 316 BC. Although it has nearly perfect agricultural land, it was an important trade route. During the Eastern Han Dynasty from 25-220 AD, the city was an important stop on the Southern Silk Road and gained a valuable reputation for its silk brocade industry.

Today's Chengdu has been susceptible to the downside of globalism: the replacement of traditional wooden architecture with humungous shopping malls, glossy commercial high rises, and apartment buildings that could house small towns. Pollution from too many cars, poor industrial control, and lack of recycling efforts lend the city a thick atmosphere, although its tree-lined streets, parks, and green spaces help. Because of its location at the foot of a mountain, Chengdu does not receive many days of full sunlight in a year.

We love the commercial street in Chengdu called Jin Li. It has been a commercial street at least as far back as the Kingdom of Shu, which began in 219 AD. At that time, the population in Chengdu was already 1,300,000! The same street is also found in historical records from the Qin Dynasty, going back to 221 BC. We love that the world's first paper money was invented and printed in Chengdu. And we love that Chengdu has a reputation as a laid-back city—the hustle and bustle of Shanghai or Hong Kong are not to be found here.

Above: The capital of the Sichuan province is an important economic leader for Western China.

Well-being	6/10
Historical role	6.5/10
Attraction	4/10
Population	9/10
Dynamism	6.5/10
Average score	6.4/10

Patrick Bonneville: Yes, Liverpool is the birthplace of pop music, but above all it is the grand port of the United Kingdom, home of the Titanic and many other great vessels. The United Kingdom wouldn't have had the impact it did on the world without Liverpool and its hard-working citizens.

Above: 1909 map of the Canning Dock. The Port of Liverpool played a vital role in UK history.
Right: Statue of John Lennon in front of the Cavern Club on Mathew Street, the bar where the Beatles were discovered.

Liverpool, England is a port city with a population of 434,900 people and just over one million when including the metropolitan regions. Known as "the Pool," its residents are called Liverpudlians or Scousers, after a popular local dish called scouse, a type of stew.

The population of Liverpool remained low until the shipping industry began to flourish here. When it did, business was not centered around the import of goods such as silks and spices; rather, it was a central port for the eighteenth-century slave trade. Many of the city's wealthiest made their fortunes from this sordid commerce.

Liverpool is 2008's European Capital of Culture, as designated by the European Union. The title came after years of restoring historic structures, building modern new spaces, and transforming abandoned factories and warehouses into trendy shops, cafés, and desirable apartments. Indeed, although many decades of post-industrial depression gave the city a grimy reputation, Liverpool has truly walked away from all that. First-class museums and art galleries dot the city—and all of them are free!

In 2004, UNESCO honored Liverpool's waterfront and docks with the title of World Heritage Site. There are more UNESCO listed buildings here than in any other city in England, except London.

Liverpudlians are proud of their Fab Four. The Beatles had their beginnings in Liverpool before they launched the British Invasion. In 1961, the world's original megagroup started their stratospheric rise at the Cavern, the Liverpool rock and roll nightclub that now calls itself the most famous in the world.

We love Liverpool for its role as a strategic port in World War II and as the shipbuilding site that produced the Titanic. We love Liverpool for its role in the new era of popular music history—music from Liverpool wasn't your mom's music; it was your music! And we love that Liverpool is home to Britain's oldest Black community, dating to the 1730s. The city is also home to the oldest Chinese community in Europe.

Well-being	8/10
Historical role	7/10
Attraction	5/10
Population	6.5/10
Dynamism	5/10
Average score	6.3/10

www.cavern-liverpool.co.uk

Patrick Bonneville: Dublin is the urban heart and soul of Irish culture and pride.

Dublin is the largest city and the capital of Ireland. In Irish, its name is *Baile Átha Cliath*. Dublin has a metropolitan population of about 1.6 million. One BBC Europe-wide survey that questioned 11,200 residents of 112 urban and rural areas voted Dublin to be the best European capital city in which to live.

Dublin has existed for about 1,000 years. Since its origins, it has been Ireland's principal city, catering to the country's educational, industrial, and cultural needs. Typically, Dublin was the town rural Irish moved to when they left their farms. The city developed without formal planning, and today many streets are narrow and seem to lack inspiration. A Dubliner, on the other hand, is not lacking in inspiration: city dwellers are full of fire, hope, and optimism.

Two important events shaped the lives of Dubliners: the Great Famine of 1845 to 1851 brought tens of thousands of deaths and even more Dubliners fled the country. It was the single greatest catastrophe in Irish history. Later, during the Easter

Left: The Ireland rugby union team.
Above: St. James's Gate Brewery, home of Arthur Guiness' famous Irish dry stout.

Rising of 1916, Irish Republicans took control of Dublin and announced the creation of the Irish Republic. After less than one week of fighting, the rebels surrendered to the superior British forces and their leaders were executed under a gloom of frustration and disappointment. Despite this disastrous blow to the independence movement, the Irish War of Independence followed in 1919, and in 1922, the Irish Free State was founded and headquartered in Dublin.

We love the friendliness and open arms of Dubliners. We love that Dublin has over six hundred pubs, including the Brazen Pub, which is Ireland's oldest, dating back to 1198. And we love Guinness beer, which Arthur Guinness began brewing in 1759. We love Dublin's youthfulness and vibrance—live music and singing are everywhere.

We love Dubliners' wild and wicked sport of rugby. The International Rugby Board is headquartered here. We love the "other" Irish sport, too: horse racing. Ireland's horse racing history is a rich as the country itself.

Well-being	7/10
Historical role	6.5/10
Attraction	5/10
Population	7/10
Dynamism	6/10
Average score	6.3/10

Patrick Bonneville: Bangkok is big, very alive, and hot—maybe too hot!

Bangkok is the capital and largest urban area of Thailand. It is known in the Thai language as *Krung Thep Mahanakhon.* The city's metropolitain population is about 12,000,000 people. There is a multicultural presence in the city, as Western, Indian, and Chinese people complement the majority Thai population.

Bangkok had the most of humble of origins, starting as a small sea town named *Bang makok,* or "village of olives," along the Chao Phraya River. When a canal was developed as a short-cut from Ayutthaya, the capital of Siam, to the sea, the city's importance grew. Trade was the major industry, as missionaries, writers, explorers, and dignitaries stopped off on their way to Ayutthaya, which, at this point in the seventeenth century, was bigger than London. As Ayutthaya grew in impor-tance, so too did Bangkok.

Above: The colorful heavy traffic of Bangkok.
Upper right: A morning at Damnoen Saduak floating market, which is now mostly a tourist attraction.

Today's Bangkok is built on its strong economy, which is boosted by the power of Asian markets and tourism. Bangkok is the gateway to the rest of the country but is also a destination in itself. With its markets, canals, and famous nightlife, there is much to see and do in town. Bangkok received the second-highest number of tourists in the world, after London. A good many of them might be visiting for Bangkok's infamous "sex tourism" trade.

We love that the full ceremonial name given to the city of Bangkok by King Buddha Yodfa Chulaloke, and later edited by King Mongkut, is listed in the *Guinness Book of Records* as the longest place name: "Krung Thep Mahanakhon Amon Rattanakosin Mahinthara Yuthaya Mahadilok Phop Noppharat Ratchathani Burirom Udomratchaniwet Mahasathan Amon Phiman Awatan Sathit Sakkathat-tiya Witsanukam Prasit." Thank heavens its citizens don't need to put all that on their envelopes!

Well-being	3/10
Historical role	6/10
Attraction	7/10
Population	9.5/10
Dynamism	6/10
Average score	6.3/10

Patrick Bonneville: Denver is in the wild, wild West. It was built because of a gold rush and is now the great outdoor city of the United States. People come for work, for the air, for the beauty, and for the mountains.

Above: Built at 1,609 m (5,280 feet) above sea level, Denver lies at the foothills of the Rocky Mountains.
Lower left: Railway connections allowed Denver to develop as the major economic pole of the region.

Denver, Colorado, has a population of nearly 600,000 people and about 2.5 million including the greater urban region. It is often called the "Mile-high City" because it is exactly one mile above sea level. It is also sometimes referred to as "Queen City of the Plains" and the "Wall Street of the West." Denver makes it onto our list of the top 100 cities because of its high ranking in natural beauty and its draw for tourists and new residents.

In the summer of 1858, eager prospectors from the state of Georgia made their way to the Rocky Mountains to find precious metal. As it turns out, gold was not very abundant, but land was. The early settlers got the best land, and before long, a town was built up, services were offered, and ideas were blooming. General William H. Larimer was not one of the earliest to arrive but he was a clever entrepreneur who bought land, laid out a city plan, and gave the place a name: Denver, after Kansas Territorial Governor James Denver.

Denver is not an international city in the same way that many others on our list are. It is, however, a unique town. Originally situated in the middle of nowhere, with no road, railroad, lake, or river, the city has an energy that can only come from the spirit of survival. Today it boasts diverse neighborhoods and a thriving downtown.

We love the views in Denver. Sitting at the foot of the Rocky Mountains, and benefitting from about 300 days of sunshine annually, the city is graced with beauty. Residents profit from the mountains in both health and economic terms, as tourists join them in skiing, hiking, climbing, kayaking, and camping.

Well-being	9/10
Historical role	3.5/10
Attraction	6/10
Population	6.5/10
Dynamism	6/10
Average score	6.2/10

ft: Located at the tip of Western Australia, Perth
the most isolated metropolitan area of the world.
low: Most of the city's skyline was built between
*75 and 1992.

Patrick Bonneville: There is something special about Perth. It might be the sun, the sea, the people, or just the fact that it is so isolated. It seems to belong to another world.

Perth is located on Australia's west coast and is the capital and largest city of the state of Western Australia. The city is home to about 70 percent of Western Australia's population, about 1,650,000 people. Perth is nestled against the Swan River and has been home to the Whadjuk Noongar people for more than 40,000 years. The area was named "Boorloo" when Europeans made first contact with the Aboriginals in 1827.

Perth joined the Federation of Australia in 1901, but only after concessions were made, including a transcontinental railway to the city, via Kalgoorlie, from the eastern states. In 1993, Perth held a referendum and voted to leave the federation; however, a new government had just taken power and basically ignored the results.

Perth is tied for fifth place in *The Economist*'s 2009 list of the "World's Most Livable Cities." It is one of the most isolated cities on earth, with the closest major town, Adelaide, some 2,104 kilometers away. Because it is so isolated, the city never really developed an international manufacturing industry. Citizens of Perth most likely work in jobs that offer some sort of service or benefit to other citizens.

With an annual average rainfall well below average, water is a precious commodity in Perth. In order to preserve and protect its water supply, the city has been very severe in controlling water consumption. It has introduced mandatory household sprinkler restrictions and created two seawater desalination plants.

We love Perth for its laid-back atmosphere and safety. We love its many uncrowded beaches. One of the most important accessories you can bring to the beach is your sunscreen—the Perth sun is hot, bright, and unforgiving.

In 1962, when American astronaut John Glenn passed over the city in the spacecraft Friendship 7, the residents of the Perth lit their house and street lights simultaneously to say "Hello."

Well-being	9/10
Historical role	3/10
Attraction	7/10
Population	6/10
Dynamism	6/10
Average score	6.2/10

Above: San Diego is built in a natural large harbor, home of the United States Navy's Pacific Fleet.

Patrick Bonneville: Lying right on the Mexican-American border, San Diego has an agreeable climate. The city of the Beach Boys seems almost perfect with its breaking waves and sunny skies.

San Diego is named after Saint Didacus, or *Diego de Alcalá* in Spanish. It has a population of over 3,000,000 people including the metropolitan region. Including its close neighbor, Tijuana, Mexico, the population jumps to 5,000,000.

In terms of American history, San Diego is not a young city. Archeological data points to life along this coast as early as 20,000 years ago. Spanish explorers arrived and settled the region in 1542. In 1602, Spanish explorer Sebastian Vizcaino named the region for Saint Didacus but adopted the Spanish name, San Diego. By 1790, about two hundred people were living in the region. San Diego was ruled by Mexico, after Mexican's independence from Spain. In 1848, after the war between the United States and Mexico, it became an American city.

We love that San Diego is a peaceful town with great weather—the United States Weather Bureau calls it the closet thing to perfect in America. We love San Diego's multicultural feel, due in part to its proximity to Mexico, but also because of its attraction for immigrants. There are more than one hundred languages represented in San Diego. We love that San Diego has one of the youngest and most educated populations in the United States: the median age is only thirty-two years, and about one-third of the workforce over twenty-five years old has at least a bachelor's degree. We also love that more than 96 percent of San Diegans are employed.

We love the great weather, sandy beaches, and other attractions that guarantee a healthy tourism industry. San Diego has one of the largest naval fleets in the world. Four navy vessels have been named USS San Diego in honor of the city.

Finally, we love San Diego for Balboa Park, a 1,200 acre (4.9 km²) National Historic Landmark urban park in the heart of the city. We love the famous San Diego Zoo that is located in the park and that has over 4,000 animals from more than 800 species. The world-famous zoo thrives on its conservation and species protection efforts.

Well-being	9.5/10
Historical role	3/10
Attraction	6/10
Population	6/10
Dynamism	6/10
Average score	6.1/10

Delhi, known locally as "Dilli," is the National Capital Territory of Delhi. It is the largest metropolis by area and the second-largest metropolis by population in India. With 12.25 million people in the city and over 15.9 million in the surrounding region, it is the eighth-largest metropolis in the world.

Until the late nineteenth century, a village named Indraprast occupied the site of present-day Delhi. The British East India company controlled the region throughout much of the seventeenth century, and after the Indian Rebellion of 1857, the Crown exercised control directly. Delhi lost the title of capital to Calcutta from 1857 to 1911, at which point the British moved the capital back to Delhi and began an important construction period. After India gained its independence from Britain in 1950, Delhi once again became the capital of India. Technically, the capital is New Delhi, which was constructed in the 1920s within Delhi's National Capital Territory.

The city features spectacular architecture, such as the Bahá'í House of Worship, popularly known as the Lotus Temple. In the setting sun, the temple looks like a giant lotus flower closing. It is a perfect illustration of expressionist architecture and has won several awards.

We love Humayun's Tomb, built in 1570 AD, and one of Delhi's three UNESCO World Heritage Sites. A second UNESCO World Heritage Site is the Red Fort of Delhi, built between 1638 and 1648, which contains gardens, halls, and a mosque. The third is the marble and red stone temple called Jama Masjid, built in 1656 by over 5,000 artisans.

It will be wonderful to see Delhi move up on our top-100 list if the city improves its quality of living. Currently, water is increasingly in short supply and the population is constantly growing. The city averages eight thousand tonnes of solid waste daily and its three landfill sites are running out space. Much of its sewage waste flows, untreated, into the Yamuna River! Otherwise, we love Delhi for its history and culture.

Well-being	3/10
Historical role	6.5/10
Attraction	5.5/10
Population	9/10
Dynamism	6/10
Average score	6.0/10

Left: Like other big cities in India, rickshaws are a popular means of transport in Delhi.

Bogotá D.C.—for *Distrito Capital,* or "capital district"—is the capital city of Colombia. Census records show the city has a population of about seven million people; including surrounding areas, it has about 8.5 million.

Prior to the Spanish Conquest, the region was a fertile basin and homeland to the Muisca, considered to be an extremely advanced pre-Columbian Indian group. Spaniards arrived in 1538 and originally named the region Bacatá but later changed it to Santa Fe de Bogotá. Locally, it was known simply as Santa Fe.

The original settlement was simply twelve huts and a chapel. The region was ruled by the Dominican Republic for a short time before falling into the hands of rulers in Lima, Peru. In 1717, Santa Fe was made the capital of a newly formed viceroyalty comprised of Columbia, Panama, Venezuela, and Ecuador. The town's pivotal role in South American affairs gave it no immunity to the earthquakes, smallpox, and typhoid epidemics that plagued the region throughout the seventeenth and eighteenth centuries. In 1821, the city was renamed Bogotá and became the capital of Gran Colombia. A railway was put through in 1884, which created direct lines to maritime routes on the Río Magdalena.

Instability shook the city on April 9, 1948, when leader Jorge Eliécer Gaitán was assassinated. The ensuing violence took the lives of 2,500 people. Later, on November 6, 1985, the M-19 Movement's revolutionary guerrillas charged upon the Palace of Justice and took over three hundred civilians hostage. Before long, one hundred and fifteen of them were dead, including eleven Supreme Court justices.

Even as recently as ten years ago, the city was one of the most violent on Earth. Today, Bogotá is making efforts to eradicate its crime-riddled image. In 1993, there were 81 murders for every 100,000 citizens; in 2007, the number of murders had dropped by nearly three-quarters. This city has apparently reinvented itself; we love that!

Bogotá might not be the first city that comes to mind when you think of the world's great cities; indeed, with its violent reputation, some may believe it's among the worst. But as the city works hard to change its reputation, the near future holds promise for Bogotá.

Well-being	4.5/10
Historical role	5.5/10
Attraction	5.5/10
Population	8.5/10
Dynamism	5.5/10
Average score	5.9/10

Left: Bogotá is located on a high plateau in the Andes at 2640 meters (8661 ft) above sea level.

Guadalajara is the capital city of the Mexican state of Jalisco and is one of the most developed in Mexico in terms of culture, trade, and economy. As of 2008, its population was 1,580,000 people, 4,300,000 including those in the metropolitan region. The city is situated at an altitude of 1,600 meters (5,200 feet).

Spanish explorer Cristóbal de Oñate founded Guadalajara in 1531, but the site of today's city was established in 1542. The original settlement was moved for several reasons, including water shortage, war, and dust storms. During the 1810-1821 War of Independence, Guadalajara was the site of the famous abolition of slavery speech by Miguel Hidalgo y Costilla. Hidalgo is often considered the "Father of the Nation," although it was Agustin de Iturbide who achieved Mexican independence.

On April 22, 1992, a devastating gas explosion plunged the city into debt, as homes, businesses, streets, and infrastructure were subjected to about a billion dollars' damage. The event was deemed accidental and it took eleven years for Guadalajara to close that chapter of its history.

We love the emphasis on culture in the city; it is especially known in the world of art and Mexicana. Recently, construction began on the Guggenheim Guadalajara, the sixth Guggenheim museum in the world.

We love that the city is home to many important educational institutions, fabulous architecture, traditional and international cuisine, and the Hospicio Cabañas, one of the oldest and largest hospitals in Spanish America. And, of course, we love that visitors can go on "tequila tours" to one of the thirty or so local distilleries of Mexico's national beverage.

"The moment of our freedom has arrived, the hour of our liberty has struck; and if you recognized its great value, you will help me defend it from the ambitious grasp of the tyrants."
—Father Miguel Hidalgo

Above: Guadalajara Metropolitan Cathedral. This city landmark has survived many earthquakes.

Well-being	6/10
Historical role	6/10
Attraction	4/10
Population	7.5/10
Dynamism	6/10
Average score	5.9/10

Patrick Bonneville: No one can argue the importance of Xi'an in the history of China and humanity. The Terracotta Army is living proof of its rich history.

Xi'an is the capital of the Shaanxi province in the People's Republic of China. It is one of the oldest cities in China and one of its seven ancient capitals. Xi'an's population is over 8 million people. The Chinese characters that create the written name mean "western peace."

With an estimated history going back some 500,000 years, this city is old! It was a cultural and political center of China in the eleventh century BC. Xi'an itself was built around 194 BC and was the capital for thirteen dynasties and seventy-three emperors. It was an important stop on the famous Silk Road and greeted explorers from across the known world. And Xi'an was already an ancient city when Jesus, Mohammad, and Siddhartha walked the earth.

Today, the city and its region boast about one hundred universities that graduate about three thousand information technology students a year. The largest Internet bar in the world is in Xi'an, with more than three thousand computers for users.

We love the world famous important archeological finds that were made in this region. In 1953, Banpo was discovered just east of Xi'an. Here, experts uncovered several well-organized Neolithic settlements that are estimated to date to about 4,500 BCE. Most famously, however, was the Terracotta Army discovery of 1974. A group of peasants digging for a well discovered the first of three pits containing a vast collection of more than eight thousand life-size terracotta soldiers, horses, and chariots. The first emperor of China, Qin Shi Huang, had ordered the mind-boggling Terracotta Army and his own mausoleum to be built, beginning in 246 BC. Some 700,000 workers spent about 400 years creating the great army. No two soldiers have the same face. They wore real clothing and all were outfitted with actual weapons. The clay figures were intended to help the emperor rule in the kingdom of his afterlife.

We love Xi'an's opera industry, with its performances of Qinqiang, the oldest and most extensive of the four major types of Chinese opera. We also love Xi'an's mountains: Hua Shan is only about one hundred kilometers east of the city and is one of China's five sacred Daoist mountains. South Peak, its tallest, reaches 2160 meters.

Well-being	4.5/10
Historical role	7/10
Attraction	4/10
Population	8/10
Dynamism	6/10
Average score	5.9/10

Right: One of the 8,000 Terracotta Warriors, each one unique and over 6 feet tall.
Right frame: Although it is more than 3 millenia old, Xi'an is a modern re-emerging city which plays an important cultural and educational role in China.

Patrick Bonneville: Mother Nature created some of the richest flora and fauna at the southwest tip of Africa, at a place called Cape Town. It is beautiful in many ways, from its natural setting to the inner beauty of its people. Things got even better when Nelson Mandela came along and enlightened the people of the region and gave hope to humanity.

Left: Table Mountain is 1,086 m (3,563 ft) high.
Above: The city has one of the most beautiful natural settings in the world.

Cape Town is known as the "Mother City" in South Africa. It has an estimated population of 3.5 million people. Residents are called Capetonians.

Although a series of European explorers had passed through the region, it was not until the Dutch East India Company created a settlement in 1652 that the region began to grow in importance. The settlement's purpose was to provide fresh water and food for the trade vessels that sailed from Asia around the cape on their way to Europe.

Europeans were cunning about exploiting the Black population, and the slave trade became extremely lucrative for those from the Northern hemisphere. By 1754, the European population here was 5,510 people, and the slave population was 6,729. When gold and diamonds were discovered in the Transvaal region, the area became extremely valuable to the ruling British society and this led to a formalized policy of segregation. On February 11, 1990, life in Cape Town changed, however: Nelson Mandela made his first public speech in decades from the balcony of the Cape Town City Hall. A new era of hope for South Africa had begun.

We love that Cape Town is the most popular international tourist destination in Africa. Cape Town has wonderful weather, amazing and diverse beaches, sports activities galore, and a good number of hiking and mountain climbing spots. The city itself is an expression of color, architecture, and joy.

We cannot love Cape Town for its prejudice and discriminatory past but we can love Cape Town for its future. We love that there has been an increase in funding to conventionally "non-white" higher education institutions. We love Cape Town for being a city that has learned from its unfortunate past and is on its way to a bright future.

Well-being	5/10
Historical role	4/10
Attraction	7.5/10
Population	6.5/10
Dynamism	6.5/10
Average score	5.9/10

Left: The Main Market Square located in the Old Town dates back to the 13th century and is the largest medieval town square in Europe.

for about six hundred years, until the city decided that gardens should take their place. Today, a large city park called Planty surrounds the historical center of Krakow.

The city was controlled by Nazi Germany during World War II and served as capital of Germany's General Government. As a result, the entire Jewish population was moved to a walled zone known as the Krakow Ghetto. Many were then moved from there to extermination camps. Thomas Keneally's book, *Schindler's Ark*, and the subsequent movie, *Schindler's List*, portray some of the horrific events that befell the residents of the Krakow Ghetto.

We love the Krakow Market Square, which has existed since 1257. We respect the city for its unfortunate role in World War II and its resilience after the fall of the Nazi regime. We love Krakow for Oskar Schindler, one of humanity's noblest men. And we love Krakow because it is a magical city. Nicholas Copernicus wandered here streets and Pope John Paul II knew its streets. Krakow is a living, breathing history book.

Krakow, Poland, has a population of 1,250,000 including the metropolitan region. Geographically, it sits within 250 kilometers of Slovalia, the Czech Republic, and the Ukraine. For centuries Krakow was the capital of Poland and home to Polish kings.

Krakow, which dates back to 966 AD, was a city that attracted scientists and artists who came to vie for the attention of the king. The beautiful monuments and buildings that still adorn the city are testaments to the legacy these citizens created.

Peace was secured for the city when it was fortified with two rows of ramparts, watchtowers, guarded gates, and a moat. Begun in 1285, the fortifications stood

Well-being	7/10
Historical role	6/10
Attraction	4/10
Population	6/10
Dynamism	6/10
Average score	5.8/10

Patrick Bonneville: From its gold rush to the end of apartheid—one of humanity's most important social revolutions—Johannesburg has become the most solid city on the African continent.

Johannesburg has a population of roughly 4,000,000 people, and over 10,000,000 including the metropolitan region. It is often referred to as "Josi" or "Jo'burg."

The city and its surrounding region have been home to humans for thousands of years. Today's Johannesburg began around 1886, after the discovery of gold; the mines at the Witwatersrand have supplied an estimated 40 percent of all the gold mined from Earth. The mine, town, and its area were controlled by the British, who did not do a very humane job of it. Their scorched-earth policy of burning crops and killing livestock devastated the people of the surrounding area. Thousands of Blacks and Boer women and children were forced into concentration camps—at least 40,000 died.

The Black population of the region had been exploited, imprisoned, and oppressed for decades, when, in 1948, the National Party took power and initiated apartheid, or segregation. This involved

Left: The city has the strongest economy of any metropolitan region in Sub-Saharan Africa. With no direct access to the sea or large rivers, the city's container terminal is the largest "dry port" in the world,

moving the majority of the Black population to Sophiatown and the South West Townships, known as Soweto.

The city has come a long way since its early days of intolerance and discrimination. Crime still remains an important issue, however. This may be due, in part, to the high unemployment rate—current unemployment is at 37 percent.

We love Johannesburg for the efforts of its citizens—the Black community, and pockets of white communities—that are committed to creating a fair and just society, free from crime, racism, discrimination, and prejudice. And we love Johannesburg for its institutions of higher learning. We love the city for its love of music and laughter. But mostly, we love Johannesburg for its good people who want to make their city safe and fun for all its citizens.

"South Africans must recall the terrible past so that we can deal with it, forgiving where forgiveness is necessary but never forgetting."
—*Nelson Mandela*

Well-being	4.5/10
Historical role	6/10
Attraction	4.5/10
Population	8/10
Dynamism	5.5/10
Average score	5.7/10

Patrick Bonneville: La Ville de Québec *is where I first discovered the meaning of the word "city." As for a first love, your first city stays carved in your heart forever, especially when it is as beautiful and as meaningful as Quebec City. This is where the English and the French had a grand battle to decide who would control North America.*

Quebec City is the capital of the province of Quebec. Its metropolitan region has a population just over 700,000 people. The name comes from the Algonquin word *kébec,* which means "where the river narrows."

Founded in 1608 by Samuel de Champlain, Quebec City is one of the oldest in North America. It was a walled city, and the ramparts surrounding *le Vieux-Québec* are the only remaining fortified city walls in North America, north of Mexico.

Well-being	8.5/10
Historical role	6.5/10
Attraction	6.5/10
Population	2/10
Dynamism	5/10
Average score	5.7/10

Above: The city is built on a solid promontory of quartz called *Cap Diamant* (Cape Diamond).

Quebec City was the place of two defining moments for British North America and New France. It is the site of the Battle of the Plains of Abraham, during the Seven Years' War, when James Wolfe led the British army to defeat the French under Louis-Joseph de Montcalm. France ceded New France, including Quebec City, to Britain in 1763. The city was the site of a second battle known as the Battle of Quebec of 1775. This time, American troops tried to "liberate" Quebec City and compel Canada to join the United States; their initiative failed.

Today, Quebec City is the French stronghold in Canada and in the Americas. The city is enhanced by its old-European style architecture, especially in the ramparts of Old Quebec.

We love Quebec City for its historic role in the building of Canada and in the fate of North America. We love Quebec City for its charm and allusions to a time long ago. We love it for its famous winter Carnaval, the largest winter celebration in the world.

Patrick Bonneville: Manila has had a restless past and will probably have a restless future. Because of its geographical location and because of its size, it is one of the most important cities in the world.

Manila is the capital city of the Philippines. With a metropolitain population of 11,500,000 people, it is one of the most densely populated cities in the world. It has several nicknames, including Pearl of the Orient, Queen of the Orient, The City of Our Affections, City by the Bay, and the Distinguished and Ever Loyal City.

Under Malay rule, in the thirteenth century, the city was known as Seludong or Selurung. Its current name is based on the nila, a flowering mangrove plant that grows along the city's marshy shores. The architecture of Manila is a concrete reminder that the city spent nearly four centuries under Spanish rule. Under the Spaniards, Manila was the seat of government from where the Philippine Islands were controlled.

In 1899, the United States purchased the Philippines from Spain as part of the Treaty of Paris; the Americans colonized the archipelago until 1946. The United States laid plans to grant the Philippines independence in 1935, but their ten-year plan was extended due to the Second World War, which brought serious ruin to the city. Manila was the second-most destroyed city in the world, after Warsaw.

We love Manila for its patience under changing rulers; the city was controlled by the Spanish, briefly by the British, the Americans, by martial law under Ferdinand Marcos, and finally under democratic rule today, following the triumphant success of Corazon C. Aquino. Aquino led the People Power Revolution and rose to power following the assassination of her husband, Senator Benigno Aquino, Jr.

Well-being	4.5/10
Historical role	6/10
Attraction	4/10
Population	8.5/10
Dynamism	5/10
Average score	5.6/10

Right: Makati City. This district of Manila is the financial and commercial center of the Philippines.

Kuala Lumpur is the capital and largest city of Malaysia. Its population stands at 1,809,699 people, 7.2 million when counting the metropolitan region. It is often simply referred to as K.L.

This relatively young and culturally diverse city is located at the junction of the Gomback and Klang rivers. It was founded in 1857, when it was basically a trade center for the tin industry. The Selangor Royal Family, under the direction of Raja Abdullah, had sent eighty-seven Chinese prospectors into the jungle to mine for tin. Although only eighteen of them survived the trip, a successful mine was established.

The flag of an independent Malaya was raised in 1957, at the end of British rule, and in 1974, Kuala Lumpur separated from the state of Selangor, in which the city is now an enclave. Skyscrapers popped up everywhere, resulting in a truly unique city that is lively and vibrant. Many older structures are being destroyed in favor of new construction, although there are some small efforts to conserve heritage buildings. The Petronas Twin Towers are marvels of modern engineering. Until recently, they were the tallest buildings in the world.

The official language of the city is Bahasa Melayu, a Malay language. Since the city's population is also composed of many Chinese, Indian, Eurasian, and other Asian people, a variety of languages are heard on Kuala Lumpur streets. The economy of the city is the backbone for the entire country. There is a large foreign presence, as multinational banking and insurance companies operate from the city.

We love Kuala Lumpur for becoming such a great city in such a short time. We love the Sultan Abdul Samad Building, which is located in front of Dataran Merdeka, or "independence square." The building has been the backdrop for many historical events, including the declaration of Malaysia's independence.

Well-being	6/10
Historical role	4/10
Attraction	4/10
Population	8/10
Dynamism	6/10
Average score	5.6/10

Upper page: Kuala Lumpur City Center Park.
Above: Malaysian Independence Day parade.

American headquarters. The city has a reputation as Brazil's trendsetter for all things arts-related – music, fine arts, literature, architecture, and theater.

We love the architecture of Belo Horizonte. The Mineirão stadium is one of the largest soccer stadiums in the world, and the São Francisco de Assis Church was designed by the Brazilian Modernist architect Oscar Niemeyer. But one of the most important reasons why we love Belo Horizonte is former Mayor Patrus Ananias de Sousa. He began a series of projects in 1993 whereby citizens were granted "the right to food." His innovations included a farmers' market in town that allowed citizens to actively survey prices across the entire city; his initiative resulted in a fair pricing scheme.

We also love that the city is working on a project to improve the quality of life for the poorest areas of the country, including initiatives to relocate those living in flood-prone regions, pave dirt roads that will increase efficient public transportation, increase police and postal services, and ensure that local families hold local jobs.

Belo Horizonte, or "beautiful horizon," is the third largest metropolitan region in Brazil. The city's population stands at 2.4 million, but it jumps to 5.4 million with the official metropolitan region.

While some settlements here date from the early 1700s, the current city was formed in the 1890s. The original founder, João Leite da Silva Ortiz, discovered that the region was perfect for farming. He established a lucrative farm and that brought people to live in the area. In 1906 the city embraced industrialization but adopted a by-law that prohibited workers from living within the urban area. As a result, infra-structures were expanded and suburban areas developed. Today, beautiful parks bursting with vegetation, birds, and mammals surround the city. For Brazilians, Belo Horizonte is a city of culture, education, and sport and a beautiful town with winding streets, hilly terrain, and tree-lined avenues.

The city has not stopped growing; many companies, such as Google, choose Belo Horizonte as their Latin

Well-being	6/10
Historical role	5/10
Attraction	4/10
Population	8/10
Dynamism	4.5/10
Average score	5.5/10

Amman is the capital city of the Hashemite Kingdom of Jordan. Currently, about 2.5 million people live in the metropolitan area of Jordan. It is one of the oldest continuously inhabited cities in the world.

Organized settlements of the region date to at least 6,500 BC. The city was called Rabbath Ammon; it was named for the Ammonites, a nomadic people who settled in the region. The Assyrians inhabited the city next, later the Persians, and finally the Greeks. When Egyptian ruler Ptolemy II Philadelphus conquered the city in about 4 BC, he renamed it Philadelphia. It remained stable for the next few hundred years, until it became part of a union of free city-states loyal to Rome. Under the Roman Empire, roads, baths, and theaters were built, and impressively engineered buildings rose from the desert. Soon, Philadelphia was the center of an important trade route joining the Mediterranean to China and India. It was a period of great wealth.

Above: Known as the "City of Seven Hills," Amman is considered by many to be the most stable city in the Middle East.

By 635 the city was conquered by an Arabic general and passed to the hands of the Muslim state of the Caliphate. This was the start of a long period of decline for the city. In 1878, the Ottomans started a village in the ruins of Philadelphia, and the Amman we know today appeared in history when Jordon become independent, in 1946.

The city has grown drastically since the start of the war in Iraq in 2003. With international business and trade looking for an alternate region, Amman was in the right place at the right time. It became an important transportation link and communications hub. Today it is a tolerant Arab city with a diverse demography and liberal convictions; it also enjoys a low crime rate.

We love the Roman Theater, built around 170 AD and restored in the 1950s. Up the hill from the theatre is the Citadel, built at the same time, and which offers a wonderful view of the city. We really love that throughout its long history, Amman has developed religious and ethnic tolerance, a rarity in the region.

"It is the Capital that courageously faced the treacherous whims of time."
—*Office of the mayor of Amman*

Well-being	5/10
Historical role	9/10
Attraction	4/10
Population	4.5/10
Dynamism	4.5/10
Average score	5.4/10

Patrick Bonneville: The city built between the two great oceans, Panama City has, because of its strategic location, played a major role in connecting the world.

Panama City is the capital and largest city of the Republic of Panama. With a population of 813,097 people, 1,206,792 including the metropolitan region, it is one of the smaller cities on our list. Despite its small size, it has had an important and historical role for humanity.

Founded on August 15, 1519, the city was originally the launching point for expeditions to South America, specifically to Peru. It also became the point of trade for gold and silver that was shipped back to Spain. The Panama Railroad Company began operating in 1855 and brought great prosperity to the city. And it was the first time travelers could make a brief trip across land from the Atlantic to the Pacific and back!

bove: Panama City is probably the most strategilly located city in the world, connecting the Pacific d the Atlantic oceans. Its prosperity is guaranteed the Panama Canal, which joins the two oceans.

The construction of the Panama Canal was the key to real significance for this area. Joining the Caribbean Sea to the Pacific Ocean, the canal gave ships a shortcut that meant they no longer had to go around the treacherous tip of South America, or, in the opposite direction, around South Africa to get from one ocean to the other. Building the canal wasn't easy: disease, landslides, and financial setbacks plagued the construction process, and an estimated 27,500 workers died during its construction. An old French crane boat, The Alexandre La Valley, made the first crossing through the canal on January 7, 1914.

A bird's eye view of Panama City today shows a beautiful skyline of high-rise condominium and office buildings and hotels. These buildings reflect the role the city has in the maritime industry and in the banking and foreign investment businesses that accompany it.

We love the tourism in Panama City. Old Panama offers a glimpse into its Spanish past through architecture and monuments. We also love Panama City's links to nature.

Well-being	5/10
Historical role	5/10
Attraction	5/10
Population	7/10
Dynamism	5/10
Average score	5.4/10

Patrick Bonneville: I hesitated a lot to include Tehran in this book. It is an important city with a very powerful history. On the other hand, a very dark shadow lies over it. There is much tension between conservatives and young citizens who would like their city to be opened to the world. The walls and the doors are still closed for the moment, but the whole world knows that beyond the rigid facade, there is a population rising for the sake of the nation and for the sake of humanity. Tehran is to be discovered. We might not see it right now, but I strongly believe it will open its arms to the rest of world.

Tehran is the capital and largest city of Iran. This heavily populated city lies at the foot of the Tochal Mountains. There are 14,000,000 inhabitants in the metropolitan region.

Its existence as Tehran is noted in some historical documents dating back to the thirteenth century. Unfortunately, war and modernization have eradicated much of the city's architecture that dates back to antiquity. Many citizens today live in high-rise apartments that were built after the Iran-Iraq war ended in 1988. These neighborhoods are often sardonically referred to as a "Tehran Identity Disaster."

Well-being	3/10
Historical role	8/10
Attraction	5/10
Population	7.5/10
Dynamism	3/10
Average score	5.3/10

Above: Tehran is surrounded by two natural barriers, the desert with temperatures reaching 50 °C (122°F) and the Alborz Mountains to the north, with summits of 5,610 m (18,405 feet).

Education has come to occupy an important place in Tehran. It has about fifty colleges and universities and is the city of choice for young adults wishing to pursue higher education. Women make up more than 50 percent of the student body. Their participation in learning, however, is subject to the strict adherence of Islamic law, which includes a dress code, gender segregation in public and harsh punishments for refusing to accept Islamic law.

We love that Tehran has many of the makings of a world-class city. We love its surprising cosmopolitan aspect, as diverse ethnic and linguistic groups animate the city. Unfortunately, the fear that drapes the city like a thick fog prevents freedom and liberty from blooming and continues to hold the city down. When Tehran breaks free from the abusive power under which it suffocates, we could see a renewed, vibrant city join the world!

We also love that in 2003, Shirin Ebadi, Tehrani lawyer, human rights activist, and founder of the Centre for the Defence of Human Rights in Iran was awarded the Nobel Peace Prize.

Patrick Bonneville: Ho Chi Minh City to locals, Saigon to foreigners and expatriates, this Asian metropolis is the heart of Vietnam. It is determined to take its place in globalization.

Ho Chi Minh City (HCMC) is the largest city in Vietnam. Its population stands at just over seven million people, although when the surrounding area is included, the population is over nine million.

Known by its Cambodian name *Prey Nokor* until the seventeenth century, the area was originally inhabited by the Khmer people. France conquered and ruled the city as part of its colony beginning in 1859, and then, in 1949, the State of Vietnam was created. After the end of the Vietnam War, in 1975, in what Americans call the Fall of Saigon, the city fell into the hands of the socialist Vietnamese People's Army and its name was changed to Ho Chi Minh City. The history of the city is painted on its architecture and monuments, and on the faces of its people. There are smiles on these faces, but for those old enough to remember, there is the pain of war.

Left: Family riding on a motorbike in Ho Chi Minh. Motorbikes are the primary form of transportation in the city.

Today, HCMC city seems electric and chaotic, a place of public bustle, secret charm, and boundless energy. It is a city full of color and optimism, with a zest for life that can only come from living through hardship. The city is driven by Vietnam's economic boom, and its growing tourism, mining, agriculture, and seafood industries are important sources of revenue.

We love the city's eighty universities and colleges and over four hundred thousand students. We love that the city has one of the most advanced health systems in Indochina.

We love to hope that Ho Chi Minh City and Vietnam in general can hang on to some of their traditional ways of life. The family unit that is so important is breaking down, as young people choose electronic avenues of communication rather than traditional theater, written, or oral traditions. If the city can find a balance between culture, tradition, and the modern world, it just might become one of the greatest cities in Asia.

Well-being	3/10
Historical role	5/10
Attraction	5/10
Population	8.5/10
Dynamism	5/10
Average score	5.3/10

Patrick Bonneville: Rare are the New World cities that are such an extraordinary marriage of culture between natives and new arrivals. Lima is the great result of the best of both worlds.

Lima is the capital and largest city of Peru, South America. With its population of 7,605,742 people in the city and 8,472,935 in the metropolitan area, Lima is the fifth-largest city in Latin America. Spanish conquistador Francisco Pizarro founded Lima in 1535 and named it *La Ciudad de los Reyes,* or "The City of Kings."

So many people make Lima their home that the city is a patch-quilt of shanty-towns, business districts, promenades, and seaside suburbs. It has the look of a developing nation and an ancient European city all melted into one. Although there is a clear middle-class society, the majority of citizens live outside this category, and many live without heat, electricity, and even running water.

"The Very Noble, Distinguished and Very Loyal City of the Kings."
—Lima's Coat-of-Arms, received from the Kings of Spain on December 7, 1537

The city moves at a dizzying pace. It is crowded, polluted, and, at times, very dangerous. The city offers multiple distractions from these challenges, however. A person can escape to the pre-Inca pyramids, wander the Spanish colonial streets, or dine on some of the best South American cuisine at restaurants. People can shop in big American-inspired shopping malls, paraglide off a cliff, or don their dancing shoes for an all-night party.

With such a large number of unemployed people, the city suffers from petty crime. Fortunately, foreigners are rarely hurt. The tourism industry brings in some revenue, but there is hope for growth in other areas, such as the high-tech industry. Since 2007, the Peruvian economy has grown 9 percent; in that same year, the Lima Stock Exchange also grew by 185.24 percent, making it one of the fastest growing stock exchanges in the world.

We love Lima and its European, Andean, and Asian influences; the city is a true melting pot of cultures. We love Lima's parks, large boulevards, and its many museums.

Well-being	5/10
Historical role	5/10
Attraction	5.5/10
Population	7.5/10
Dynamism	3.5/10
Average score	5.3/10

Right: The Plaza Mayor is the birthplace of the city and the heart of Peru.

Left: Residential apartments. Due to rapid growth in recent years, the disposable income of the city's residents has increased by 50% in just 5 years.

Below: The growing landscape of Guangzhou.

Located about 120 kilometers northwest of Hong Kong, Guangzhou merits a spot on our list because of its business dynamism. It is home to about 6.3 million people, nearly 10 million when including the surrounding areas. It is the third-most populous metropolitan region in mainland China. Once upon a time, Western society referred to the region as Canton; its food and language are still known as Cantonese.

The history of the area dates to 214 BC. By 226 AD, the region was known as Guangzhou and its capital city was Panya. In 1918, the city's urban council declared Guangzhou to be its official name. The city rapidly developed as an important port during the opium trade and remained so until China put an end to the illegal activity. Following both world wars, the city turned to manufacturing. The promise of jobs brought hundreds of farmers to the city looking for factory work, and as the last century came to a close, African emigrants flooded to Guangzhou looking for work. Today, at least one hundred thousand Africans live in the city, and some reports say this number increases by 30 percent annually.

Guangzhou is an important city for Chinese foreign trade and business and is the site of China's largest trade fair, the Canton Fair. Despite its reputation as a city for work, not play, we see a city that values traditional Chinese culture. Stroll down any typical backstreet and you will see friends and family playing games, drinking tea, and talking.

We love Guangzhou for the Pearl River Tower. According to project engineers, the tower will be the most energy-efficient building in the world and the tallest tower in China. It is scheduled to open in 2010. We love the city's urban park—the largest in China. We love that Guangzhou is a liberal, prosperous, and cosmopolitan city.

Well-being	5/10
Historical role	5/10
Attraction	3/10
Population	8/10
Dynamism	5/10
Average score	5.2/10

Patrick Bonneville: Because it is one of the oldest cities in the world, Alexandria is one of the greatest.

Alexandria is the second largest city in Egypt, with a population of 4.1 million. It is home to the country's largest seaport, which processes about 80 percent of Egypt's imports and exports. This city does not have a history—it *is* history!

Above: Citadel of Qaitbay, dating from 880 AD.

Alexandria was founded by Alexander the Great in 331 BC and was the capital of Egypt for almost one thousand years. It was home to Pharos, the famous lighthouse that was one of the seven wonders of the ancient world. The lighthouse was built in the third century BC by Ptolemy I and was a magnificent engineering achievement that was built using considerable slave resources. The structure was composed of three stories, measuring between 115 and 150 meters high. It would have been one of the tallest structures of its time, second only to the Great Pyramid of Giza. The lighthouse is no longer standing, but its memory shines on. Alexandria was also home to the largest library in the ancient world and to the catacombs of Kom el Shoqafa, one of the seven wonders of the Middle Ages.

Well-being	2/10
Historical role	9/10
Attraction	3/10
Population	7/10
Dynamism	4/10
Average score	5.0/10

Alexandria is a port town that has survived sieges, bombings, attacks, and occupation. Today, the city shows the marks of time, yet it is aging gracefully. The beaches are popular, and many restaurants and cafés provide a perfect spot for people-watching. It is humbling to walk on ground that may once have been graced by Alexander the Great, Ptolemy, Cleopatra, Julius Caesar, Mark Antony, Napoleon and Omar Sharif, to name just a few.

We love Alexandria for withstanding centuries of war and natural disasters. We love that Alexandria remained Egypt's capital city through the Hellenic time, under Roman rule, Byzantine rule, and Persian rule. We are sorry that more remnants of the great old city did not survive, although Pompey's Pillar still stands.

We love that the new library, Biblioteca Alexandrina, sits on the site of the ancient Library of Alexandria. And, finally, we love the Corniche, the fifteen kilometer walkway that follows the harbor and is dotted with restaurants, markets, and historic sights.

Left: The world's largest civilian administrative building, the Palace of the Parliament. Built in the 1980s, the 1,100-room building is a heritage of the Soviet era and the Ceauşescu regime.

Patrick Bonneville: Called Little Paris for a long time, this city is like no other because of its architecture. From the Middle Ages, to the Communist legacy, to the modern era, these witnesses to history are everywhere in Bucharest.

Bucharest is the capital of Romania, and with its population of two million people, it is the country's largest city. It is also the industrial and financial center of Romania.

The site of present-day Bucharest dates back to 1459. By 1862, it was a well-established center that served as the hub of Romanian culture and trade. Bucharest was occupied by various forces throughout its history. During World War II, Bucharest was part of the Axis empire of alliances against the Allied Forces and consequently sustained heavy losses. After the war, Romania and Bucharest were governed by Nicolae Ceauşescu's communist regime until the late 1950s. The country suffered greatly under the Soviet banner

and under Ceauşescu; historical records show that hundreds of thousands of civilians were tortured, killed, or disappeared during this period.

By the time the Communists left Hungary, Bucharest was greatly diminished. Many of its historic districts were destroyed and replaced with generic, big-box housing units. Today, however, Romania has entered a period of economic revival: technical advances, modern media, and an increase in development are creating an urban renewal. The city has a low unemployment rate of only 2.5 percent and is one of the safest European capitals. It also boasts one of the Continent's biggest and most efficient transit systems. The city has challenges: a significant corruption problem pervades institutions, and there is an unfortunately high number of street children.

We love Bucharest for its Romanian history and culture. Bucharest is a city in transition and for those who call it home, a city of hope.

Well-being	5/10
Historical role	6/10
Attraction	5/10
Population	4/10
Dynamism	5/10
Average score	5.0/10

Havana, Cuba, is officially called *Ciudad de La Habana*. It is the capital city of Cuba, as well as the main port and commercial center for the country. The Havana urban region has a population of 3.7 million, which makes it the largest city in the entire Caribbean region.

Architecture in Old Havana draws its inspiration from baroque and neoclassic styles. *La Habana Vieja,* or "Old Havana," is the core of today's city. Buildings hug one another on the winding, narrow streets of this colonial sector that was established in 1519. The neighborhood grew rich from shipbuilding and as a stopover from the Old World to the New World.

Tourism is the primary source of revenue for Havana and for Cuba. Prior to Fidel Castro's communist regime, Havana was the Caribbean's most popular destination. While the United States was in the constraints of prohibition, Havana was not. It was an easy and laid-back city for rich Americans to visit, where leisure was more important than work.

Following World War II, American organized crime controlled an important chunk of Havana's tourism, and the island became an important base for the illegal drug trade. In 1959, the Cuban government created the National Institute of the Tourism Industry and regained control, although with the 1961 trade embargo against Cuba, the tourism industry fell into dire straits. It was only in 1982 that Fidel Castro decided the time was right to reinvent tourism for Cuba. He went in search of foreign capital in order to develop his revitalization project, and by the end of the twentieth century, Cuba and Havana relied on tourism for revenue more than on any other industry.

We love Havana because as far as culture goes, no other city in the Caribbean offers as much for its citizens and for its tourists.

Before the rise of communism, Havana cinema was recognized as one of the best in the world. Although the Cuban regime put an end to the glory days of that industry, we hope time will fix this. We love the fifty or so museums housing everything from renaissance to modern art, sculpture, and new media.

We love to hope that the new era of government in both the United States and in Havana will bring renewal to Cuba. Havana is an optimistic city that is just aching to thrive in the new millennium.

Well-being	3/10
Historical role	7.5/10
Attraction	5.5/10
Population	6.5/10
Dynamism	2/10
Average score	4.9/10

Patrick Bonneville: Because of its petro-dollars, Riyadh is of arch significance to the world. This is the city where religion, politics, and economy morph into one. Despite its wealth and good international relationships, the city might become a challenge for the rest of the world.

Riyadh is the capital and largest city of Saudi Arabia and is home to close to six million people. Its name is a derivative of the Arabic word *rawdha,* meaning "garden."

The history of Riyadh goes back to before the birth of the Islamic religion, around 630 AD. When the modern kingdom of Saudi Arabia was established in 1932, Riyadh was made its capital.

Riyadh is one of the world's fastest growing cities. Its area has grown more than one hundred times its original size in the past fifty years, and its population has jumped from 20,000 to almost 4.5 million.

While the city has the charm of ancient ruins and picturesque markets, Riyadh—Saudi Arabia—is a place of political and social paradox. While Saudi Arabia and the United States carefully cultivate diplomatic relations and economic alliances, there is a growing current of radical Islamic activism in the city and country that means repression for women, intolerance of other religions, and brutal punishment for criminals.

We love Riyadh's ancient ruins and vast parklands, and its rise in the modern economy. Above all, we love the debates it generates all around the world, especially about human rights and women's rights. We hope that Riyadh will take giant steps in these two domains to serve as a model for the Middle East.

Well-being	4.5/10
Historical role	7/10
Attraction	3.5/10
Population	7/10
Dynamism	2.5/10
Average score	4.9/10

Far left: Disabled car in front of the monument to the revolution in Havana.
Left: Kingdom Centre, also known Burj Al-Mamlaka, a symbol of the weath and modernism of Riyadh.

Above: View of Jerusalem from the Mount of Olives. The Old City's walls were built in the 16th century under the Ottoman reign.

Patrick Bonneville: In every book I write or publish, I try to make a statement about Jerusalem when the subject fits. I try to say that it is very unfortunate that this city does not live up to its aspirations. It is the most meaningful city for three of the biggest religions humanity has ever known, yet it seems to be a place of bloodshed, confrontation, sorrow, and hate. This city might never be at peace. I just hope we can help Jerusalem change its fate. I just wish Jerusalem could live up to what it is supposed to be, according to all religions.

Jerusalem is the capital and largest city of Israel. It has a population of some 760,000 people, and just over one million including the metropolitan region. One of Earth's oldest cities, it is a sacred site for many of the world's great monotheistic religions, including Judaism, Christianity, and Islam.

While the city figures on our list because of its rich history and spiritual significance, we do not condone the violence that haunts its streets, leaks from its borders, and permeates its soul. We want Jerusalem to be a model city, a city of acceptance and forgiveness, a city of faith and pride. Unfortunately, in these, it is sorely lacking.

Nevertheless, a walk through Jerusalem reveals one of the most intriguing cities on the planet. Even for those of other faiths, or no faith at all, the presence of religion is remarkable. Down one street is the Christian Church of the Holy Sepulchre, down another is the Western Wall with its devoutly praying Jews, and down yet another is the Al-Aqsa Mosque. At last count, the city had 1204 synagogues, 158 churches, and 73 mosques. In the course of its 6,000-year history, the city has been destroyed twice, besieged twenty-three times, attacked fifty-two times, and captured and recaptured forty-four times. Roughly calculated, that represents one major disruptive event every fifty years—and yet we dare to hope for peace!

Jerusalem offers a good quality of life to the majority of its residents, all things considered. We love the city's excellent restaurants and markets and cultural festivals, including the Jerusalem Film Festival which screens both Israeli and international films. Families can visit the Biblical Zoo; almost every pair that was on Noah's Ark is in this zoo. Visitors can see Hezekiah's Tunnel, with its knee-deep water and the Pool of Shiloah—it is said that Jesus cured a blind man in these waters. The Israel Museum welcomes close to one million visitors each year, as does Yad Vashem, Israel's memorial to the victims of the Holocaust. It houses the world's largest library of Holocaust-related material.

Above: Walking through time in the Old City. Most of Jerusalem's landmarks are located in this small part of the city, including the Temple Mount, the Western Wall, the Church of the Holy Sepulchre, the Dome of the Rock and al-Aqsa Mosque.

We love the efforts of interfaith groups that work for peaceful relationships and justice on the ground in Jerusalem, such as Jerusalem Peacemakers. We love the annual Jerusalem Hug as a symbolic gesture to unite all the world's groups.

Well-being	3/10
Historical role	10/10
Attraction	4.5/10
Population	5/10
Dynamism	2/10
Average score	4.9/10

Patrick Bonneville: This is a very meaningful and important place for many people in our world. I am not a religious man, but I cannot deny the role Makkah plays for humanity.

The Saudi Arabian city Makkah is the holiest meeting site of the Islamic religion. The population is 1.7 million people in the city and about 2.5 million including the surrounding areas. It is the birthplace of the Islamic prophet Muhammad and the religion he founded. The Saudi Arabian government has requested that the official spelling be Makkah, rather than Mecca.

Once a year, between two and four million Muslims from the world over perform the Hajj pilgrimage that brings them to Makkah. The Hajj is an obligation for every Muslim to perform, provided they have the means to do so. Pilgrims descend on the city of Makkah for about seven days for a series of prayers, a show of solidarity, and submission to Allah. Non-Muslims cannot enter Makkah. There are no exceptions.

Well-being	1/10
Historical role	7/10
Attraction	8/10
Population	7/10
Dynamism	1/10
Average score	4.7/10

Upper right: The Qur'an was revealed to Muhammad by the angel Jibrīl (Gabriel) near Makkah.
Right: The Kaaba, heart of the Hajj, the largest annual pilgrimage in the world.

Makkah places in our top 100 cities because of its significance for the roughly 1.57 billion Muslims on Earth. It has been said that the city spends the entire year preparing for the next Hajj. A 2008 study on the long-term effects of participating in the Islamic pilgrimage found that the Hajj experience opens the lines of communication between Muslims and followers of other religions. The event promotes peace and equality.

Regrettably, Makkah is not a "global" city in any current sense of the word.

We love Makkah because it is so important for such a large portion of humanity. We love that the city tries to accommodate so many visitors during the short Hajj week.

PHOTO CREDITS

PHOTO CREDITS

144	Jose AS Reyes/Shutterstock	173	André Klaassen/Shutterstock
145	Colman Lerner Gerardo/Shutterstock	174 b	Asier Villafranca/Shutterstock
146	Ilja Mašík/Shutterstock	175	Joris Van Ostaeyen/Dreamstime.com
147	Chris Sargent/Shutterstock	176 b	MAWHYYOUARE/Shutterstock
147 b	Tmcfarlan/Dreamstime.com	176	Douglas Litchfield/Shutterstock
148	Bhowe/Shutterstock	177	Warren K. Leffler
148 b	Nzgmw2788/Dreamstime.com	178	Chris Curtis/Dreamstime.com
149	Rick Lippiett/Dreamstime.com	179 b	piotr beym/Shutterstock
150	Mcarter/Shutterstock	180	Dmytro Hurnytskiy/Shutterstock
153	James Arevalo/Dreamstime.com	180 l	Artur Bogacki
153 b	Eet0013Dreamstime.com	180 b	Laurent Dambies/Dreamstime.com
154	S.Borisov/Shutterstock	181	Joanna Redesiuk/Dreamstime.com
156 b	Felix Mizioznikov3Dreamstime.com	182 b	Javarman/Shutterstock
157	Richard Goldberg/Shutterstock	182	Birute Vijeikiene/Shutterstock
158	Redsquarephoto/Shutterstock	183	José Marafona3Dreamstime.com
158 b	Pontus Edenberg/Dreamstime.com	184	Elwynn/Dreamstime.com
158	Matthias Straka/Shutterstock	184 b	Iloveotto/Dreamstime.com
159	Vlas2000/Shutterstock	185	Michael Chien/Dreamstime.com
159 b	Leshik/Shutterstock	186	Masr/Dreamstime.com
160 b	Rebekah Bentley/Shutterstock	187 l	Tyler Olson/Dreamstime.com
161	7505811966/Shutterstock	187 b	Duncan De young/Dreamstime.com
162	Sam Chadwick/Shutterstock	187 r	Cyberlot/Dreamstime.com
162 b	Jiri Flogel/Shutterstock	188	Filip Fuxa/Dreamstime.com
163	Jackson, W. Henry. Detroit Publishing Co	190	Mikhail Nekrasov/Shutterstock
164	Emei/Dreamstime.com	190 b	Chad McDermott/Shutterstock
164 b	Emei/Dreamstime.com	191	Bertrand Collet/Shutterstock
165	Gary718/Shutterstock	192 b	T-Design/Shutterstock
165 b	Roger Jegg/Shutterstock	192	Christoffer and Peter Suhr
166	Pastushenko Taras/Shutterstock	193	Antoine Beyeler/Shutterstock
166 b	Natalia Bratslavsky/Dreamstime.com	194 b	Merttu/Dreamstime.com
167	Dmytro Korolov/Shutterstock	195	Ruta Saulyte/Dreamstime.com
168 b	Alan Merrigan/Shutterstock	196	Gabor Racz/Shutterstock
168	Warren Goldswain/Shutterstock	197	Kristian Sekulic/Shuttestock
168 b	Gemenacom/Shutterstock	197 b	Tomasz Szymanski/Shutterstock
169 b	Gary718/Shutterstock	198 r	Gary Yim/shutterstock
169	Unknown	198 b	Gemenacom/Shutterstock
170 b	Jbor/Shutterstock	198 l	Tifonimages/Dreamstime.com
170	Loggan11	199 b	Neo3721/Dreamstime.com
171 b	Greg Henry/Shutterstock	199	Alexandercai/Dreamstime.com
171	Andre Nantel/Shutterstock	200 b	Wong Yu Liang/Shutterstock
172	Paul Prescott/Shutterstock	200	Zhu Difeng/Shutterstock

201	VanHart/Shutterstock
201 b	Fabrizio Zanier/Dreamstime.com
202	David Lochhead/Shutterstock
202 b	Pontus Edenberg/Shutterstock
203	Jean Morrison/Shutterstock
204 l	Vladimir Melnik/Shutterstock
204 b	Absolut_photos/Dreamstime.com
204 r	Absolut_photos/Dreamstime.com
205 l	Veronika Bakos/Shutterstock
205 r	Tedholt/Dreamstime.com
205 b	Regien Paassen/Dreamstime.com
206 b	Jakez/Shutterstock
206	Ed Willmann
207 b	Feng Hui/Dreamstime.com
207	Feng Hui/Dreamstime.com
208	Ant Clausen/Shutterstock
210 b	Sean Gladwell/Shutterstock
210	Bristish Admiralty
211	George Groutas
212	Eoghan McNally/Shutterstock
213	Jamt9000
213 b	Abdone/Dreamstime.com
214 l	Dmitry Kushch/Shutterstock
214 r	Juriah Mosin/Shutterstock
214 b	Pontus Edenberg/Dreamstime.com
215 r	Nick Lamb/Shutterstock
215 b	Kelly Bates/Dreamstime.com
215 l	Steve Keller/Dreamstime.com
216	Gemenacom/Shutterstock
217	Alexander Sakhatovsky/Shutterstock
217 r	Andrew Geraghty/Dreamstime.com
218 b	Sebastien Burel/Shutterstock
218	Photoquest/Dreamstime.com
219 b	Paul Prescott/Shutterstock
219	Paul Prescott/Shutterstock
220	Graham S. Klotz/Shutterstock
220 b	Dario Diament/Dreamstime.com
221 b	Posada, José Guadalupe
221	Holger Mette/Dreamstime.com
222 b	Darren On The Road
223 l	Fly/Shutterstock
223	Harley Couper/Shutterstock
224	Jacques Kloppers/Dreamstime.com
225	W. Woyke/Shutterstock
225 b	Mark Soskolne/Dreamstime.com
226	Novvy/Shutterstock
227 b	Sean Gladwell/Shutterstock
227	MikeE/Shutterstock
228 b	Massimiliano Pieraccini/Shutterstock
228	Martin St-Amant
229	Holger Mette /Dreamstime.com
229 b	Holger Mette /Dreamstime.com
230 b	Miskani/Dreamstime.com
230 ur	Shirley Hu/Dreamstime.com
230 lr	Ijansempoi/Dreamstime.com
231	Gabriel Nardelli Araujo/Dreamstime.com
231 b	Adam Golabek/Dreamstime.com
232 b	Dario Bajurin/Dreamstime.com
232	Alex_saveliev/Dreamstime.com
233 b	Gemenacom/Shutterstock
233	Afronova/Shutterstock
234	Joel Blit/Shutterstock
234 b	Ruslan Gilmanshin/Dreamstime.com
235	Mark Soskolne/Dreamstime.com
236	Carlos E. Santa Maria/Shutterstock
236 b	Manuel González Olaechea y Franco
237 l	Xiaowei Xu/Dreamstime.com
237 b	Fallsview/Dreamstime.com
237 r	Hsc/Dreamstime.com
238 b	Ahmed Aboul-seoud/Dreamstime.com
238	Karim Farah/Dreamstime.com
239 b	Sean Gladwell/Shutterstock
239	Insuratelu Gabriela Gianina/Shutterstock
240	Jeff Whyte/Dreamstime.com
240 b	Adambooth3Dreamstime.com
241	Salem Alforaih/Shutterstock
241 b	Tomas Marek/Dreamstime.com
242	Dejan Gileski/Shutterstock
242 b	Aron Brand/Dreamstime.com
244 b	Monkey Business Images/Dreamstime.com
244	Paul Cowan/Dreamstime.com
245	Ahmad Faizal Yahya/Dreamstime.com

*"Divine Nature gave the fields,
human art built the cities."*
—Marcus Terentius Varro